How To Invest Money With God

PURPOSE AND DEDICATION

There are many books written today on giving, yet there are still many unanswered questions in the minds of people. For this reason I have written this book in Questions & Answers to encourage Christians to believe God and receive the blessings that God wanted and intended for them to have.

I dedicate this book to my faithful and loving husband, Rev. William Clayton, whose encouragement has enabled me to share with him in minisry. And to our two daughters, Diana and Miriam, who have shared with us through the years that God is our source, whether in times of plenty or in times of want. We can say with hearts filled with thanksgiving that our Heavenly Father was faithful and met our every need.

HOW DO I KNOW
THE TITHE MEANS ONE-TENTH?

Webster: "The tenth part of anything; a tax of one-tenth, especially collected to support churches."

Stewards of Tithing

Thirteenth Edition 1991

Copyright © 1954, Rev., Christal Clayton

Copyright © 1984

Permission must be obtained in writing for the reproduction or copying of any portion of this book.

CHRISTOS PUBLISHING COMPANY, INC.

31630 Railroad Canyon Road, Suite 5, Canyon Lake, CA 92380
1-800-676-2035

Foreword

My appreciation for Christal Clayton's ministry to the whole Body of Christ is based on the biblical balance with which she addresses the subject of stewardship, and the covenant convictions which motivate her appeal to every believer to partner with God's plan for our practical, personal and financial blessing.

She avoids the tinsel of superficial or carnal ideas about prosperity and cuts to the core of the vital issues of God's Truth — Truth which sets us free from sinful negligence and selfish fear and into a joyous experience of His intended blessing at every dimension of our lives.

I commend her book to all who have a need for such a solid Bible-based teaching on tithing and giving.

Jack W. Hayford, *Pastor*
Church on the Way
Van Nuys, California

Contents

Part I   Page
Introduction — What is Stewardship?........................ 7
  1. What is the office of a steward?........................ 8
  2. How long has the plan of tithing been in existence?........ 8
  3. Wasn't tithing given under the Mosaic law?................ 8
  4. To whom does my money belong, God or me?............ 10
  5. Will people in this day accept the plan of tithing?.......... 11
  6. Is money a curse?.................................... 11
  7. Why should believers tithe?........................... 12

Part II
  1. Would a man rob God?................................. 13
  2. How can a man rob God?.............................. 14
  3. How much of our tithe do we have to bring?............... 14
  4. Where does the tithe belong?.......................... 15
  5. Why do we bring our tithe?........................... 15
  6. When should we bring our tithes?...................... 16
  7. Does God leave any question unanswered?............... 16
  8. How can I know if I tithe that all my other needs be met?... 16
  9. If my husband is unsaved how do I tithe on all the income?..... 17
 10. If I tithe should I expect an increase?..................... 17
 11. What is the result of paying our tithe and giving our offering?.... 18
 12. What did God mean when He said, if we pay our tithe He
     would open the windows of Heaven?..................... 18
 13. If if faithfully pay tithes, yet adversity still persists, what should
     I do?.. 19
 14. If I pay my tithes does it mean I will never have any
     financial troubles?................................... 19
 15. How far should a Christian go in seeking to increase
     his material blessings?............................... 20
 16. What should be our basic motive for tithing? 21
 17. What should be our attitude toward our money?........... 21
 18. Why should the wicked prosper?....................... 21
 19. If I am upset with my pastor, may I withhold my tithes?..... 22
 20. What is the result of not paying tithes?.................. 23

Part III
  1. May we borrow our tithe?.............................. 24
  2. If I pay my bills, there is no money left. How can I tithe?.... 24
  3. Can I pay part of my tithe?............................ 25
  4. Will a person who does not tithe lose out on the blessings
     of God?... 25
  5. Can I wait till I get out of debt to tithe? 26
  6. I want to tithe, but there are so many things I need.
     Won't God understand? 26
  7. Does God hold us responsible for vows?................. 26
  8. Does the United States government recognize tithing? 26
  9. Does God need our tithe? 27
 10. Who should tithe?.................................... 27
 11. Should you send your tithe to a radio or television
     broadcast? 27

12. Should a minister tithe on his income? 27
13. Should we pay our tithe through the envelope system?...... 28
14. Should a minister do secular work?......................... 29
15. Did Jesus or the Apostles do away with tithing? 29
16. What did Jesus say in regard to tithing?.................... 29
17. Does Jesus praise anyone for tithing?...................... 30
18. If Jesus fulfilled the law, then why should I tithe? 31
19. If tithing is not a financial problem, what kind is it?........ 31
20. If I don't tithe, how will it affect my church? 31
21. Is tithing for the New Testament age? 32
22. Was tithing practiced by the New Testament church? 33
23. As a New Testament Christian, have we been "liberated"
    from the practice of tithing?................................ 33
24. Is there a difference between legalistic performance and
    that of loving obedience?................................... 34
25. How is God's wisdom displayed in our tithing?.............. 35
26. What is the New Testament plan for the support
    of the church?.. 35
27. Should tithing be a test of church membership?............. 36
28. Should all of our giving be to the church?.................. 36
29. If I am one of the larger tithers in the church, should I have
    more to say in regard to spending its finances?.............. 37
30. Would tithing of all the members solve the church's
    financial problem?.. 37
31. What does the bringing of our tithes and offerings do for
    the church? 37
32. Does the church need money?.............................. 37
33. Is it necessary for members of a local church to bring their
    tithes into their own church treasury?...................... 38
34. Wouldn't voluntary giving be more acceptable to man than
    tithes and offerings? 38
35. Why does the church always lack money? 39
36. Can I give part of my tithe to help support relatives, or a
    charity organization?....................................... 39
37. Why doesn't the church take care of all the poor?........... 39
38. Should the poor be encouraged to give?.................... 40
39. Who promised to pay us back if we give to those in need? 40

Part IV
1. What is the spiritual side of tithing?......................... 41
2. Is tithing in any way responsible to Christian growth?....... 41
3. If I only work part time, and my salary will not support my
   family, should I tithe?....................................... 42
4. Should someone tithe while in debt?........................ 42
5. If we say everything we have is the Lord's, then why do
   we say one tenth is the Lord's?.............................. 42
6. Should we pay tithe before deducting our current expenses?... 42
7. Can I deduct Social Security and Income Tax before
   paying my tithe?.. 43
8. After I tithe, am I responsible for what is left?.............. 43
9. Should gifts received by legacies be tithed?................. 43
10. How can one tithe without any certain income?............. 43

11. If I am buying my home, why can't I deduct my payments before tithing?.................................... 43
12. What is the difference between tithing the income and the increase?.. 44
13. What is the net income?.................................... 44
14. Do I tithe on my gross earnings or my take-home pay? 44
15. Is tithing compulsory? 45

Part V
1. What is the difference between tithes and offerings?........ 46
2. Did God charge that we robbed Him in tithes only?........ 46
3. How much offering should we give?...................... 47
4. To what extent does God expect me to give? 47
5. Why Is It So Hard For Some People To Part With Their Tithes And Offerings?.................................... 48
6. Why Is Everyone Today Looking For Security?.............. 48
7. Why has the joy gone out of taking offerings in the church? 49
8. Why must our giving be accomplished through love?........ 49
9. Why must I give in order to worship God? 50
10. What will happen when we give?......................... 50
11. What will happen if we don't give? 51
12. What does our love for God have to do with our giving?..... 51
13. Why does God want and expect me to give?................ 52
14. Should Christians make a will? 53
15. Is giving to world missions a part of the tithe?.............. 53
16. If God chooses to bless and prosper me, does he have any requirements on how I am to use the money? 53
17. Why do some Christians say, "I don't want any of this world's goods"? 54
18. Is it a sin to have good things? 54
19. Do we have a right to claim God's promises regarding money and expect to receive them?....................... 55
20. Is it wrong for a Christian to be rich? 55
21. Can a Christian have a bank account? 55
22. Should a Christian invest, save or hoard for the future?...... 56
23. What is God's program in regards to giving?................ 56
24. Is getting our needs met conditional or unconditional? 57
25. Does God want His servants to prosper?.................... 57
26. Is tithing the solution for all church finances?.............. 58
27. Is there only one place where Jesus endorsed tithing? 58
28. Why should we give cheerfully? 59
29. Why is Satan called the devourer? 60
30. What is the difference between the benefits of Satan and of God? 61
31. Why does God want His children to have money?.......... 61
32. Prosperity Scriptures? 61
33. Some noted tithers?.................................... 62
34. When the heart is right, what will be our response to tithing? 63
35. Covenant of fulfillment?.................................... 63

Part I

WHAT IS STEWARDSHIP?

Stewardship is our heritage as sons of God. It reaches into every phase of our Christian life. We are God's stewards over all things that he entrusts into our care such as time, talent, faith and service.

Ministers of the gospel many times are prone to neglect the financial phase of the church, but this is not possible nor advisable, because God's blessing is only promised to the church that is obedient to His will. It is not enough to simply get enough money to operate the church, but it is more important for people to realize that it plays a very necessary part in their worship.

The first thing we must understand is that a Christian is a steward and not an owner. This is the hardest part to make clear as many professing Christians claim ownership over all that they have and even speak of "giving" their tithe — whereas the Bible calls it "paying" God's tithes.

There are others that are very careful to pay their tithe but after that, they feel whatever is left is theirs to use in any way they choose. But if Christians today would study God's word, they would become convinced that all they have belongs to God, that they have no claim except as a steward to hold and dispose of it as it would be pleasing to God.

When a faithful steward realizes that the method of tithing is literally that of taking one-tenth of his income and depositing it in the Lord's treasury, he will be glad to do it, instead of feeling that whoever appeals to him for the work of God is trying to get his money away from him. Rather, he will feel that everyone who presents to him the interests of God's kingdom is helping him to find a way to discharge his obligation to God.

Jesus called his Ministers to be stewards of truth and one phase of that stewardship is in relation to money. Just as one must preach repentance with much emphasis and repetition, so also must he preach on the money question frequently.

You will reap more than you sow;
God will return to you in multiplied form.

1. WHAT IS THE OFFICE OF A STEWARD?

Literally, a steward is the guardian of the interests of another. The steward owns nothing, but is careful to guard, protect, and increase the property of the one whom he serves. It is true that we are stewards of our time, talent, strength, and ability as well as our money. But our faithfulness in tithing is in reality the greatest test of our stewardship because the fleshly nature desires money more than anything else, that it might be exalted.

2. HOW LONG HAS THE PLAN OF TITHING BEEN IN EXISTENCE?

The principle of tithing began in the garden when God made Adam and Eve stewards over it. He gave them access to all the garden, but He reserved one tree for Himself. We must realize that even though Adam and Eve had dominion over it, they could not partake of it, for it was God's. When they disobeyed Him and partook of that which He had reserved for Himself, He drove them out of His garden. God has never relinquished His claim, for He declared, Psalms 24:1 "All the earth is mine." God took one day out of seven and set it aside for His church, and one-tenth of the money of His people for the furtherance of His kingdom. And wherever you find people keeping God's system and giving one-seventh of their time, and one-tenth of their income, you will see churches filled with people, the treasury filled with money, and God-s blessing resting upon that church, because this is pleasing unto the Lord. By keeping one day in seven holy, you will find you are guided by the Lord the other six; because when we sanctify one day, the other six are blessed of the Lord. Likewise when we are faithful to bring in our tithes and offerings, He will guide us in what to do with the rest.

3. WASN'T TITHING GIVEN UNDER THE MOSAIC LAW?

No, Abraham brought "tithes of all" (Genesis 14:20) 500 years before the Mosaic law was given. Two hundred years later and three hundred years before Moses, we hear Jacob making a covenant with God *"And of all that thou shalt give me I will surely give the tenth unto thee."* (Genesis 28:22) Abraham, long before the law was given to Moses on Sinai, realized he was

Tithing, a biblical minimum:
It will not limit our giving, but open the door
to a genuine stewardship.

only a steward over all he possessed. He tithed unto Melchizedek as priest of the Most High God. *"To whom Abraham gave a tenth part of all."* Hebrews 7:1-9

In Psalms 110:4 is a prophecy concerning Christ, "Thou art a priest forever after the order of Melchizedek." The seventh chapter of Hebrews leaves no question in our minds who Melchizedek really is, because Hebrews 7: 2 & 3 describes Melchizedek as the "King of Righteousness, King of Salem, which is, King of Peace." The Scripture declares that He had no beginning, no ending, "but made like unto the Son of God; abideth a priest continually." Jesus did not do away with, abrogate (or annul) the law; instead He fulfilled it. By this, we realize that the establishing of the concept of tithing was so important to God that He established the tithing principle five hundred years before He established the Mosaic Law. Abraham is called the father of the faithful, being justified by faith. For this reason the gospel begins in the faith of Abraham, who rejoiced to see the day of Christ and he saw it with gladness. We are the seed of Abraham by faith in Christ. "And if ye be Christ's, then are ye Abraham's seed, and heirs according to the promise." Galatians 3:29

If Abraham practiced tithing when he only saw Christ through faith, how can we who have enjoyed the reality of the gospel do less? "If ye are the seed of Abraham, ye would do the works of Abraham." Abraham was not only a faithful tither, but he saw to it that God received his share first before any of the young men received their part. "He paid tithes of all."

If you are tempted to feel that tithing was just an Old Testament custom and does not apply to your New Testament experience, then please note the facts: It was practiced by Abraham for over five hundred years before the law was given. Abraham was not only justified by faith, but he proved his faith by his works, and paid tithes to God's priest. You ask, where did Abraham get the idea of tithing? Genesis 14:22, "I have lifted up my hand to the Lord, the Most High God, the Possessor of heaven and earth." Abraham was a true steward. He knew that God owned all things, that He possessed heaven and earth, therefore that He was justified in claiming the tithe of all. The principle of tithing was recorded in the first book of the Old Testament and then re-established in the New Testament in

Tithing, a Christian witness
Consistent giving before the community
is one of the evidences of Faith.

the book of Hebrews, to establish that this principle of God's Righteousness is good for all dispensations.

The law which came five hundred years later cannot do away with the righteousness that went before. If God intended to do away with His tithing system, why did he charge His people with robbing Him of His tithe? Why would He promise to curse them if they failed when He declares, "He changes not."

4. TO WHOM DOES MY MONEY BELONG, GOD OR ME?

Not only did God own the Garden, He owns all things. He declares in Psalms 24:1 "The earth is the Lord's and the fulness thereof; the world, and they that dwell therein." Psalms 50:10-12 "For every beast of the forest is mine, and the cattle upon a thousand hills. I know all the fowls of the mountains: and the wild beasts of the field are mine. If I were hungry, I would not tell thee: for the world is mine, and the fulness thereof." Haggai 2:8 "The silver is mine, and the gold is mine, saith the Lord of Hosts."

One of the first things we must realize is that our existence and whole economic system depend not upon industry, but upon the soil from which life comes. For if we did not have food, we could not exist no matter what else man was able to produce. In order to meet our needs, all we do is till the ground. Then the question we must answer is, Who gave the seed? — God. Who gave the fertile soil? — God. Who makes the sunshine? — God. Who makes the rain fall? — God. Most land owners that go into partnership demand at least one-half or one-third. But God provides all, even to giving us our health and strength. And what does man do? He plants and tills God's soil, and all God asks in return is one-tenth. When man transgressed God's law, he lost everything. But when Jesus redeemed him, He paid the price for us in full. "Ye are bought with a price" (I Corinthians 6 :19& 20) under the gospel. We have no right to call anything our own, not even ourselves.

Tithing, an acknowledgement of ownership:
That God is owner of all and I am only
a steward or trustee over my human estate.

5. WILL PEOPLE IN THIS DAY ACCEPT THE PLAN OF TITHING?

II Timothy 4:3 & 4. , "For the time will come when they will not endure sound doctrine; And they shall turn away their ears from the truth, and shall be turned unto fables." Yet in the church we accept the blood of Christ and its power to wash away our sins, or the Holy Spirit, or Water Baptism, or any other of the commandments of God. Why then should we reject tithing when it is not our program, but God's, and is the one thing that will bring prosperity to His children.

First, the tithe made possible the support of His ministry. Second, the tithe was His plan for giving financial security to His people. To compare the tithe to everyday life would be to compare it to an insurance policy. Failure to keep up the premium would cause the policy to lapse. Likewise our failure to pay our tithes cancels God's obligation to provide financial security for the defaulter.

III John 2. "Beloved, I wish above all things that thou mayest prosper and be in health, even as thy soul prospereth." It is God's will that all of His children prosper. But the secret is that with every promise God gives, there is a condition we have to meet. Then and only then is God obligated to fulfill His promise. You will notice we have to take the first step in faith, then God steps in and proves Himself.

6. IS MONEY A CURSE?

No, it is a blessing if it is used for the glory of God. His word says, I Timothy 6:10 "The love of money is the root of all evil." When money becomes our desire and we put it ahead of doing the will of God, then it is sin. Luke 16:13 "Ye cannot serve God and Mammon"; that is, money. Notice it is not God or Mammon, but God and Mammon. When we are working so many extra hours just to make money, that we don't have time to put God's work first in our life, money has become our god and will separate us from a life pleasing to Him. Remember He wants our time as well as our money. Jesus speaks of various grades of stewardship, the "wicked and slothful servant" or steward, and the "unfaithful steward," and then of the

Tithing, a token of consecration:
That we have surrendered all and
made Him Lord.

11

"faithful," who shall have his heavenly reward. Someone said: "He i
not rich who lays up much, but he is rich who lays out much." God'
treasury is man's opportunity.

7. WHY SHOULD BELIEVERS TITHE?

1. It is God's plan handed down to us in His Word.
2. It was endorsed by Jesus.
3. It is the only practical business-way for us to recognize God's prior
   claim on our time, energy and ability.
4. It will enrich our lives spiritually.
5. It brings financial blessing.

Because giving is an expression of our love, love is action.

It means moving out of self into the way of God. It is when we give
that we find the most satisfaction in our own lives, because God
created us after His own image—and God is on the giving hand. We
feel most like God when we do things like God, when we give, and
give. ·

God has not ordained us to failure. "That God who begun this
good work in you" will carry it on until it is finished. He never fails
and will never let us down." Remember this: the man who plants
few seeds will have a small crop; the one who plants many seeds
will have a large crop. Each one should give, then, as he has
decided, not with regret or out of a sense of duty, for God loves
the one who gives gladly. And God is able to give you more than
you need, so that you will always have all you need for
yourselves and more than enough for every good cause." II
Corinthians 9:6-8 (Good News for Modern Man) Jesus Himself
told us, "Freely ye have received, freely give." Matthew 10:8 The
whole Christian principle is based on giving. God proved His
love by giving His Son (John 3:16). Jesus proved His love by
giving His life (John 1:12; Romans 5:8; II Corinthians 8:9). As His
children we are to express our love the same way by giving. But
you must remember—

Never doubt in the dark what God has shown you in the light.
What is worse, a child afraid of the dark, or a man afraid of the
light?

Part II
MALACHI 3:8-10

"Will a man rob God? Yet ye have robbed me. But ye say, Wherein have we robbed thee? In tithes and offerings. Ye are cursed with a curse: for ye have robbed me, even this whole nation. Bring ye all the tithes into the storehouse, that there may be meat in mine house, and prove me now herewith, saith the Lord of hosts, if I will not open you the windows of heaven, and pour you out a blessing, that there shall not be room enough to receive it."

1. WOULD A MAN ROB GOD?

(Webster) Rob — "To steal; deprive of something rightfully owned."

Yes, man is doing it continually with no fear of the wrath and judgment of God. Robbing God is a heinous crime. (Webster) "Heinous, is atrocious, or wicked in the highest degree, outrageous." To rob God in His presence and with His knowledge is unthinkable, especially for those that claim to know and love Him. Hebrews 4:13 "But all things are naked and open unto the eyes of Him with whom we have to do." You no doubt will agree that no one would be so foolish as to rob his Heavenly Father, his benefactor, or the hand that feeds him.

Rob means "to defraud". In trying to defraud God we only defraud ourselves. The eagle who robbed meat from the altar set fire to her own nest from the burning coal that adhered to the stolen flesh. Men who retain God's money in their treasuries will find it a losing proposition. No man ever lost by serving God with his whole heart, or gained by serving Him with half a heart. We may compromise with our conscience for half the price, but God will not endorse it. Like Ananias and Sapphira we shall lose not only what we thought we had purchased so cheaply, but also the price we paid for it. Thieves may sometimes elude punishment. But the question is,

Tithing, a symbol of dedication:
We tithe not legally but lovingly,
Love always gives.

"Who can escape from Him whose eye never slumbers or sleeps?"

However, God is longsuffering. He receives no pleasure from human sufferings — even when a person suffers as a result of his own misdeeds. If we want God to open His treasury, we must first open ours.

2. HOW CAN A MAN ROB GOD?

There is no mistake, God answers this question Himself. "In tithes and offerings." Notice: It is not just tithe, but tithes and offerings. Many have been faithful in paying their tithes and feel they have paid their obligation to God, but they seem to overlook the fact that God says we have robbed Him in offerings, too. He doesn't accuse the people of neglecting their duty. He doesn't suggest that they have not been liberal enough. He says, "Ye have *robbed* me in tithes and offerings."

If our Federal Government has the right to levy a tax on our incomes, surely God who gives us time, energy and ability and provides the materials with which we earn those incomes, has a perfect right to claim a definite part of them for His work.

We may think we are gaining wealth by stealing God's money, but God keeps books; one day He will collect and when He does, it will be with compound interest!

3. HOW MUCH OF OUR TITHE DO WE HAVE TO BRING?

"Bring all the (the whole) tithes into the storehouse." It doesn't say a part, or as much as you feel led, but all. He also says it is our obligation to bring them. There are some denominations that take the tithe out of the employee's check before the employee receives the check. That of course, is up to them, but they are being robbed of the real blessing of making the choice of whether or not they want to be faithful unto God. It is true we pass offering plates and try to get that part of the service over with as quickly as we can because we feel today people get offended, but in reality that is why many churches are suffering financially today. They have neglected to teach their people the joy of worshipping God with money. We have failed to realize that it is as much a part of our worship as singing a

Tithing, a starting point for giving:
It opens the door to larger giving.

14

hymn or the saying of a prayer. Our hearts should be rejoicing as **we** bring our tithes and offerings, because it gives us an opportunity to show our appreciation to Him for all of the blessings He has bestowed upon us.

4. WHERE DOES THE TITHE BELONG?

"Bring ye all the tithes into the storehouse" (Malachi 3:10) or the church that you are a member of or attend. "Storehouse" is singular, not plural "Storehouses". The storehouse or the church is like a foundation, while television, missions, giving to the poor, are the walls, or extended hands reaching out to help minister to the world. But if you do not have a strong foundation, the walls will disintegrate because the church is the supply line. God is a God of order. He has a perfect program. He said, "Bring" not "Send".

THE CHURCH — is to do a job that television could never do — that is to minister and meet the needs of the local church body whether in life or in death.

WHILE TELEVISION — is doing a job that the local church can never do. It is going into homes of people that would never enter a church. People are being saved that the church would never reach. Such as those in hospitals or the elderly that are unable to go to church. They are being fed, strengthened and encouraged. God is not interested in just building the local church, but in building His kingdom, and His kingdom includes reaching a lost world. When the church program includes building His kingdom, God will bless and prosper the local church.

5. WHY DO WE BRING OUR TITHE?

"That there might be meat in mine house." Meat means spiritual food and Mine House as stated clearly means God's house. If we put the spiritual body first, we can always trust God for the material needs. It simply means that we must bring our tithes and offerings to the house where we go to worship God. It doesn't mean that I can send my tithes to some other church or minister I feel that is in need. You don't go to one grocery store and get your groceries and then go down the street to another store that you feel needs help and pay

Tithing, an adventure in blessing:
An opportunity to "Prove God."

them. Of course not. Besides that would be against the law and so it is against God's law. It simply means you pay where you eat. If God lays a burden on your heart for someone or some place and you feel God wants you to give to them, then give them an offering above your regular tithes and offerings. God will richly reward you for it.

6. WHEN SHOULD WE BRING OUR TITHES?

I Corinthians 16:2 "Upon the first day of the week let every one of you lay by him in store, as God hath prospered him." This shows us we are to bring our tithes and offerings regularly and systematically. Also a definite proportion of our income must be taken into consideration if we are to give as God hath prospered. The Old Testament required a certain portion of their income, while the N.T. requires that and much more. There are those that use "Christian liberty" as an excuse for not giving systematically. The word "tithe" (in the Old Testament or New) is not legalistic but a term with the meaning of systematic giving (II Corinthians 8:1-9, especially Verse 8).

Our privilege is to demonstrate righteousness by our giving. It is not something we acquire or earn. But our faithful support of the tithe becomes a continuous, joyous overflowing of everything we have.

7. DOES GOD LEAVE ANY QUESTION UNANSWERED?

No. — **How much?** — Bring all (our tithe).

Where? — To the storehouse.

Why? — That there might be meat in mine house.

When? — On the first day of the week.

8. HOW CAN I KNOW IF I TITHE THAT ALL MY OTHER NEEDS WILL BE MET?

When a child is adopted into a family, that family must prove that it can provide for that child. When God says we are adopted into His family (Romans 8:15 & 16), it means He has promised to take care and provide for our every need.

Luke 12:22-32 "And he said unto his disciples, Therefore I say unto you, Take no thought for your life, what ye shall eat; neither for the body, what ye shall put on. The life is more than meat, and the

Tithing adds Love to our living,
Grace to our giving, and
Power to our praying.

body is more than raiment. Consider the ravens: for they neither sow nor reap; which neither have storehouse nor barn; and God feedeth them: how much more are ye better than the fowls? And which of you with taking thought can add to his stature one cubit? If ye then be not able to do that thing which is least, why take ye thought for the rest? Consider the lilies how they grow: they toil not, they spin not; and yet I say unto you, that Solomon in all his glory was not arrayed like one of these. If then God so clothe the grass, which is today in the field, and tomorrow is cast into the oven; how much more will He clothe you, O ye of little faith? And seek not ye what ye shall eat, or what ye shall drink, neither be ye of doubtful mind. For all these things do the nations of the world seek after: and your Father knoweth that ye have need of these things. But rather seek ye the kingdom of God; and all these things shall be added unto you. Fear not, little flock; for it is your Father's good pleasure to give you the kingdom."

9. IF MY HUSBAND IS UNSAVED, HOW DO I TITHE ON ALL THE INCOME?

In the event he will not tithe and you have only a specified allowance with which to run your household, then you are responsible to tithe only on the moneys that come into your hands.

10. IF I TITHE SHOULD I EXPECT AN INCREASE?

The answer is found in God's law of sowing and reaping. This means we can expect a harvest from every seed we plant. Only what a farmer sows can produce his harvest, and only what a Christian gives can provide his abundant return. Note: Unplanted seed can never increase! But the harvest is always abundantly more than the amount of the seed planted. God allows most Christians to go through special times of testings. We should not go around always expecting to become possessors of wealth overnight. There must first come the forsaking of all. Abraham had to be willing to leave all before he received all. For it is only in the hard places that we learn to lean heavily on God.

Unfortunately there are many Christians who are in poverty

Tithing, an expression of gratitude:
One of the ways of expressing our thanks
to God for all His Goodness to us.

because they have allowed Satan to take advantage of them. They have not realized the Lord . . . has pleasure in the prosperity of his servants. Psalms 37:25. He created all the earth's wealth for the prosperity of those that do His will. No good thing is withheld from them that walk uprightly.

11. IF I AM BUYING MY HOME, WHY CAN'T I DEDUCT MY PAYMENTS BEFORE TITHING?

Malachi 3:10 "And prove me now herewith, saith the Lord of hosts, if I will not open you the windows of heaven, and pour you out a blessing, that there shall not be room enough to receive it." The natural man says: "Lord give unto me first then I'll give unto you." God says, "Give unto me first then I'll give unto you." He also says "Prove Me." It is the only place in the Bible where God makes man a promise, then backs it up with a challenge, "Prove Me." You ask how big a blessing can come out of the windows. When God was pouring out His wrath in the time of Noah, it was big enough to cover the entire earth. But He says when He pours out His blessings there shall not be room enough to receive it. It promises temporal blessings, Proverbs 3:9 & 10; 11:24 & 25. But it may come in many ways: spiritually, physically, as well as financially.

12. WHAT DID GOD MEAN WHEN HE SAID, IF WE PAY OUR TITHE HE WOULD OPEN THE WINDOWS OF HEAVEN?

He promised He would pour out a blessing that there would not be room enough to receive it. Does this mean only financial blessings? No. It would be like a house without windows, the air would become stale and stuffy. The reason God says He wants us to give, is so He can open the windows of Heaven and illuminate our soul. The air He sends thru the windows will drive out the spirit of covetousness, and flood your soul with a joy and peace that money cannot buy. Also the blessings He speaks of here can be health, protection, love of our family. Proverbs 13:7 *"One man considers himself rich, yet has nothing (to keep permanently); another man considers himself poor, yet has great (and indestructible) riches."* (Amplified translation).

Just as the stars guide the navigator,
so tithing gives direction to our giving.

Notice, He has also promised to rebuke the devourer for your sake. Whether a pestilence for crops or sickness that devours the weekly budget or frost that would destroy an early crop, regardless of the form of the devourer, God has promised to rebuke him for your sakes. *II Corinthians 9:6-8, "And God is able to make all grace abound toward you; that ye, always having all sufficiency in all things, may abound to every good work."*

13. IF I FAITHFULLY PAY TITHES, YET ADVERSITY STILL PERSISTS, WHAT SHOULD I DO?

Claim the promise of *Malachi 3:10 & 11* and believe God to rebuke the devourer for your sake as He has promised in *Exodus 23:25;* and *Psalms 105:37.* He has made us a three-fold promise in *III John 2, "Beloved, I wish above all things that thou mayest prosper* (material) *and be in health* (physical), *even as thy soul prospereth"* (spiritual). God declares, *"I am the Lord. I change not."* Therefore His divine ordinances are still in force.

14. IF I PAY MY TITHES DOE IT MEAN I WILL NEVER HAVE ANY FINANCIAL TROUBLES?

No. Not any more than it would mean, that if you were a child of God you could never get sick. There are three kinds of sickness just as there are three kinds of financial trouble. (1) The sickness that Satan attacks us with. (2) The sickness that we bring upon ourselves, because we break the natural laws of God by not taking care of our bodies, such as not getting proper rest, food or sleep. (3) So it is with finances. Satan brings all kinds of financial reverses to make us doubt God. There are financial troubles we bring on ourselves, when we foolishly misuse our money and run up bills, and try to blame God for our not being able to pay them. Then there are financial reverses that God sends our way to test us to prove whether we are profitable or unprofitable stewards. *"Enjoy prosperity whenever you can, and when hard times strike realize that God gives one as well as the other — so that everyone will realize that nothing is certain in this life." (Ecclesiastes 7:14) "The good man does not escape all*

*Tithing, real dedication,
is evidence that you are trusting Him completely
with your money as well as your life.*

troubles — *he has them too, but the Lord helps him in each and every one". (Psalms 34:19 - Living Bible)* Someone might ask, if we are still going to have financial trouble even though we tithe, then how does it benefit us? The difference is, if we have been faithful to Him in the time of plenty, in the time of need we can come to Him with faith and assurance that He will supply all our needs. *"Beloved, if our heart condemn us not, then we have confidence toward God. And whatsoever we ask, we receive of Him, because we keep His commandments, and do those things that are pleasing in His sight." (I John 3:21 & 22)*

15. HOW FAR SHOULD A CHRISTIAN GO IN SEEKING TO IN-CREASE HIS MATERIAL BLESSINGS?

The size of a man's pocketbook in no way indicates his spiritual status. The Apostle Paul must have run into this same error of teaching in his day when he penned these words in I Timothy 6: 5, "Supposing that gain is godliness: from such withdraw thyself." For the truth is that many have lost their experience with God in their race for material gain. II Kings 5:15-27 shows us how Gehazi and his descendants paid with leprosy because of his greed. Many Christians reason as to how much they could do if they had a great deal of money. On the other hand, they never consider the warnings of the Bible concerning the dangers of those who have large possessions. In the parable that Jesus gave in Luke 8: 14 He showed that those with riches usually brought no fruit to perfection. The "thorns" were "the cares of life and the deceitfulness of riches." The reason is that they had come to trust in riches and their time and energy was diverted from spiritual things.

On the other hand, the Bible does show us that a Christian can be a man of wealth. But we also must note that such wealth never comes to a Christian because he has pursued riches. We note in Mark 10:28-30 that Jesus told His disciples that because they had left all to follow Him, that they would "receive an hundredfold now in this time . . . and in the world to come, eternal life." This promise is still to those who are willing to leave all and follow Him. No matter how much God may bless His people with material blessing, He wants His people to be in daily dependence on Him.

Tithing: The joy of partnership with Christ.

20

16. WHAT SHOULD BE OUR BASIC MOTIVE FOR TITHING?

For material gain, no. Even though Malachi 3:10 promises us that blessing, to tithe for that blessing alone will only bring us in the end sorrow and leanness of soul. Our real reason should be our gratitude to our Heavenly Father for His mercy and His gift of salvation. Those who are faithful tithers will witness, with one accord, that they have been blessed in all areas of life: socially, financially and spiritually.

17. WHAT SHOULD BE OUR ATTITUDE TOWARD OUR MONEY?

One of the words that came to have a real meaning for us during the last war was the word "priority." We learned that the things most important to the war effort had to come first and be given right away over everything else.

From Genesis to Revelation God is trying to show us we are to put Him first and give Him first "priority" in every phase of our lives. In Matthew 6:25-33 Jesus said, "Seek ye first the kingdom of God, and his righteousness" and He promised that He will provide the other things according to our need.

For many of us the most difficult thing of all to surrender is our money. That's easy to understand because in a very real sense the money we earn is our lives converted into dollars. It represents our time, our energy, our ability, and our life's blood, as it were — minted into a coin.

When we face up to these facts, we must realize that our money isn't ours at all in any lasting sense. We did not bring it into the world when we came, and we can't take it with us when we die; more than that we can't even be sure of keeping it while we live. For sudden unexpected reverses can sweep it all away without any warning. In the final analysis, then, money is simply something that God entrusts to us and allows us to use during our lifetime.

18. WHY SHOULD THE WICKED PROSPER?

When we serve God and are faithful in our giving, yet we see the unbeliever prospering, it is hard for us to understand. If we get our eyes on him, it will become our downfall, and we will become like David and begin to doubt God's fairness and faithfulness. In Psalms 73:3 David said: "Truly God is good to Israel, even to such as are of a

Tithing seals your Love.

clean heart. But as for me, my feet were almost gone; my steps had well nigh slipped. For I was envious at the foolish (arrogant) when I saw the prosperity of the wicked." In Verses 4-12 he tells of their prosperity: "They increase in riches." They add house to house and land to land, and even dare challenge God. In Verse 13-16 David tells how he had tried to live a righteous life, and had oftentimes been plagued and chastened, while the wicked had been prospering. Many times they lived to an old age, and when they died they seemingly died in peace. But David didn't stop to think that you can't always tell man's eternal abode by his departure. It pained him to the point that he was ready to give up. What changed his mind? When he went into the sanctuary to meditate, God showed him there were two sides. Verse 17, "Until I went into the sanctuary of God; then understood I their end." Here David is brought face to face with the fact that this world is not our home, that we are only pilgrims passing through. Verses 18-20 describe their end. "They are utterly consumed with terrors. . . . Thou shalt despise their image." Verses 21-27 describe the life and the end of the righteous. After David saw the completed picture in Verse 28, he declares: "But it is good for me to draw near to God: I have put my trust in the Lord God, that I may declare all thy works." Psalms 37:10 & 11, 16-18 & 28; Malachi 3:13-15. (Read Psalms 73- *Paraphrased Living Bible.*)

19. IF I AM UPSET WITH MY PASTOR, MAY I WITHOLD MY TITHES?

Who told us to bring in our tithes and offerings to the storehouse? God. Malachi 3:10 "Bring all the tithe into the storehouse". Who said if we didn't we had robbed Him? God. Malachi 3:8 . . . "Yet ye have robbed me". If we withhold our tithe it will show that our spirit and motive is not right. Even if the pastor gets the message, so will God and it will cause Him to take His blessing off of our lives no matter how right we think we are. I Chronicles 16:22 "Touch not my anointed and do my prophets no harm".

*Give according to your income, lest God
make your income like your giving.*

20. WHAT IS THE RESULT OF NOT PAYING TITHES?

Malachi 3:9 "Ye are cursed with a curse: for ye have robbed me, even this whole nation." He doesn't say we have robbed the church, but He says "Me." This explains why some have had such a degree of sickness, doctor bills and unemployment. "Ye are cursed with a curse." God has chastened nations with famine, scarcity, unseasonable weather, insects that ate up their fruit. He chastened His people for not building the temple, and for not maintaining it. In Acts 8·20 when Simon sought to buy holy things with money, Peter cried, "Thy money perish with thee . . . thou hast neither part nor lot in this matter; for thy heart is not right in the sight of God." Simon, remembering the awful judgment that overwhelmed Ananias and Sapphira, begged Peter, "Pray ye to the Lord for me, that none of these things which ye have spoken come upon me." We may think we are getting wealth by stealing God's money, but God keeps books; and although He doesn't have a pay day every Saturday night, He will collect. When He does collect, it will be with compound interest. The natural man does not want to tithe or to give offerings because he is dominated and governed by his fleshly, carnal mind, and to him it is foolishness (Romans 8:7 & 8). To the natural man, tithing does not make sense because he has not looked into God's financial planning and been released into a new dimension of God's financial liberty.

A CHEERFUL GIVER

I've formed a partnership with God.
It's free of all expense.
He furnishes all the capital,
And I get nine-teenths.
He gives me wisdom, guidance, strength,
And power for all details.
I pay one-tenth for all of that.
My partner never fails.

"God loveth a cheerful giver" — *II Corinthians 9:7*

*God's bank remains open
regardless of the circumstances.*

Part III

1. MAY WE BORROW OUR TITHE?

Yes, but if we do, there are two penalties that we will have to pay. First, while we have it borrowed we are under God's curse, and usually so many things go wrong that we feel we can never get out of debt. Second, in order to pay it back we have to add one-fifth which is twenty percent on the tithe we borrowed. Leviticus 27:30 & 31 "And all the tithe of the land, whether of the seed of the land, or of the fruit of the tree, is the Lord's: it is holy unto the Lord. And if a man will at all redeem ought of his tithes, he shall add thereto the fifth part thereof." God's banking system is just as real as any bank here on earth. You can't borrow from any bank and not expect to pay their interest. God's rate of interest is much higher than any bank, because He wants to discourage us from borrowing it. For when we do, we often get so far behind we become discouraged and give up.

When we rob God or borrow our tithe, it not only affects us financially but also spiritually.

2. IF I PAY MY BILLS, THERE IS NO MONEY LEFT. HOW CAN I TITHE?

God never said he wanted your left-overs. He said He wanted your first fruits. Proverbs 3:9, 10. "Honour the Lord with thy substance, and with the first fruits of all thine increase: So shall thy barns be filled with plenty, and thy presses shall burst out with new wine." All through the Old Testament God required them to bring the first fruits or the firstling of the flock without spot or blemish for His sacrifice. When God redeemed man, He used the firstfruits of heaven, or the best that He had, without sin — His only son. God never requires anything of us, that He has not already done Himself. God wants the first fruits of our time, our heart, our love. He declares, "I'll have no other gods before me." He wants the first of our lives. He wants us, not just when we're old, but in our youth, and in our homes that He might be the head of our house. God wants the first fruits of our money as well, because the fruit that is left on the tree till the end of the season, usually falls to the ground and no one wants it.

God's bank remains open
regardless of the circumstances.

3. CAN I PAY PART OF MY TITHE?

You can, but that is not tithe until you have paid all of it because tithe means one-tenth. You are just as cursed for owing God one dollar as you are if you owe Him ten dollars. It isn't the amount that makes you a thief, but the fact that you took that which didn't belong to you.

Acts 5:1-11   when Ananias and Sapphira decided to say they sold their land for so much, when they really sold if for much more, Peter asked, "Why hath Satan filled thine heart to lie to the Holy Ghost and keep back part of the price of the land? While it remained, was it not thine own? And after it was sold, was it not in thine own power? Why hast thou conceived this thing in thine heart? Thou hast not lied unto men, but unto God." The thing we forget is that man cannot damn our soul, but God can. God struck them both dead, and "Great fear came upon all the church, and upon as many as heard these things." We ask ourselves the question, "Why isn't God striking people dead today?" He is, spiritually. Usually one of the first signs you will notice when a person begins to backslide outwardly, is that he will stop tithing. (Of course he has already backslidden in his heart.) "The fear of the Lord is the beginning of wisdom."

4. WILL A PERSON WHO DOES NOT TITHE LOSE OUT ON THE BLESSINGS OF GOD?

James 4:17 "He that knoweth to do good, and doeth it not, to him it is sin." Any sin, no matter how big or how little, will separate us from God if we continue to do what we know is wrong and refuse to repent and get right with God. Many times people will say, "I pray, but God does not hear my prayer." I wonder if we cannot find the answer in Psalms 66:13   when David cried out in despair, "I will pay thee my vows." Also, in Psalms 66:18 , "If I regard iniquity in my heart, the Lord will not hear me." In James 4:3 "Ye ask, and receive not, because ye ask amiss, that ye may consume (spend) it upon your lusts (in your pleasures)."

You possess, but God owns. You are God's,
so all you have is God's.

5. CAN I WAIT TILL I GET OUT OF DEBT TO TITHE?

If you do, you will have a long and hard pull. Jesus said in Matthew 6:33 "But seek ye first the kingdom of God and his righteousness and all these things will be added unto you." You will find that nine-tenths of your income with God's blessing on it will go farther than ten-tenths with His curse.

6. I WANT TO TITHE, BUT THERE ARE SO MANY THINGS I NEED. WON'T GOD UNDERSTAND?

Luke 12:15, 20 & 21. "And he said unto them, Take heed, adn beware of covetousness: for a man's life consisteth not in the abundance of the things which he possesseth. But God said unto him, Thou fool, this night thy soul shall be required of thee: then whose shall those things be, which thou hast provided? So is he that layeth up treasure for himself, and is not rich toward God."

7. DOES GOD HOLD US RESPONSIBLE FOR VOWS?

So many people make vows or pledges when money is being raised for a building program or some other church project. Then something comes along that they want or think they need, and they forget all about their vow. But first of all may we remember there is no blessing in giving to God if we haven't been faithful in paying our tithe first. Because "Obedience is better than sacrifice." Ecclesiastes 5:4&5 "When thou vowest a vow unto God, defer not to pay it; for He hath no pleasure in fools: pay that which thou hast vowed. Better is it that thou shouldest not vow, than that thous shouldest vow and not pay." God blessings rest upon those that pay their vows.

8. DOES THE U.S. GOVERNMENT RECOGNIZE TITHING?

Malachi 3:9 "Ye are cursed with a curse: for ye have robbed me, even this whole nation." Our nation was founded upon the word of God. Therefore the federal government will allow up to thirty percent deduction on your income tax. It is advisable that records be kept by the local church for government verification.

If all we have is God's property,
Satan is the trespasser.

9. DOES GOD NEED OUR TITHE?

Does God need tithe for himself, when he already has all things. Psalm 50:10-12 "For every beast of the forest is mine, and the cattle upon a thousand hills. I know all the fowls of the mountains: and the wild beasts of the field are mine. If I were hungry, I would not tell thee: for the world is mine, and the fulness thereof."

The tithe giving is needed only by man, for it is only when we give that we can receive. Psalms 50:14 & 15 goes on to say, "Offer unto God thanksgiving; and pay thy vows unto the most High: And call upon me in the day of trouble: I will deliver thee, and thou shalt glorify me."

10. WHO SHOULD TITHE?

Saint and sinner alike. The difference is that the sinner can only receive temporal blessing down here, while the Christian gets double dividends on his investment. We collect down here and then we will also collect up there, because we are laying up treasures in heaven where there will never be a bank failure.

11. SHOULD YOU SEND YOUR TITHE TO A RADIO OR TELEVISION BROADCAST?

The only one that should send his tithes to a radio or television broadcast is the person who is an invalid or who is bedfast and it is impossible for him to go to church, with the exception where the station or broadcast is owned or maintained by your local church, and is a part of the ministry of the church. Then the radio or television broadcast becomes the storehouse where he receives his spiritual meat. This is no excuse for those who just stay at home, for the Word tells us to "Bring ye all the tithes" and "Forsake not the assembling of yourselves together." If you want to see God's word go forth and reach souls and the radio or television is a blessing to you, send in an offering. God will bless you for it. It is His work. It will reach souls that cannot be reached any other way.

12. SHOULD A MINISTER TITHE ON HIS INCOME?

Yes. The Levites who received tithes were in turn expected to tithe of their income. Numbers 18:26, Hebrews 7:9.

You earn, but God enables.
God owns everything.

13. SHOULD WE PAY OUR TITHE THROUGH THE ENVELOPE SYSTEM?

When we are doing business with God and we are keeping our account straight, we do not object to the envelope system. Some people use this scripture found in Matthew 6:1-4 (Verse 3) *"But when thou doest alms, let not thy left hand know what thy right hand doeth."* Notice this is not in reference to tithe but alms, and there is a difference. *Webster says: "Alms is money given and distributed for relief of the poor and needy."* In other words we are not to go around bragging about what we have done to help those in need, but God who sees us in secret will reward us openly. Some wonder what right the pastor has to know what their tithe is. There are many reasons. Jesus is the great Shepherd and He appointed the minister as His under-shepherd, making him responsible for the sheep that God has entrusted into his care.

Hebrews 13:17 "Obey them that have rule over you, and submit yourselves: for they watch for your souls, as they that must give account, that they may do it with joy, and not with grief; for that is unprofitable for you." The minister is responsible to see that you accept Christ, are baptized in water, take communion, and go on to a deeper experience with God. The commandment of tithe is no different from any other of God's commandments. You do not become offended if your pastor talks to you and encourages you to be baptized. Why then should you be offended when he speaks to you about your tithe, for anything that has to do with God's business is his business. The envelope system gives the church an idea of how many of their people are tithing, and how much of a budget the church is able to take on. Also the pastor knows whether his church is just a tithing church or whether his church is also a giving church. A pastor has no way of trying to meet the need unless he knows what the need is.

Another important thing is that this is the only way the local church has to keep records which enable them to give out income tax receipts at the end of the year. Also, it shows that you are co-operating with the financial system in your local church, and God always blesses co-operation and unity in His people.

God will never be a debtor to any man.
No one ever outgives God.

28

14. SHOULD A MINISTER DO SECULAR WORK?

No. But many have felt they have been forced to. When God's people fail in keeping one commandment, the other part of God's plan fails too. When the church as a whole does not bring in their tithes and offerings into His house it is only reasonable there is not enough to meet all the obligations of the church and the minister also.

Paul tells us in I Corinthians 9:13 "Do ye not know that they which minister about holy things live of the things of the temple? and they which wait at the altar are partakers with the altar?" He explains here that the priesthood were supported by the tithes, then he adds in Verse 14 "**Even so hath the Lord ordained that they which preach the gospel should live of the gospel.**" The minister should live from the tithes of the people, and those who receive the gospel should gladly give this support through their tithes and offerings. God has chosen, anointed, and set him aside that he might have the time to study and shew himself approved of God rightly dividing the word of truth. The reason we bring our tithe into God's storehouse is that there might be meat in His house, and there cannot be any spiritual meat except when the pastor is there to serve it. *(Malachi 3:10)*

15. DID JESUS OR THE APOSTLES DO AWAY WITH TITHING?

Oscar Lowery says:

"It is hardly possible when one verse out of every six in the New Testament deals with the question of money and covetousness. We also find that one-half of the Lord's parables refer to the subject of money."

16. WHAT DID JESUS SAY IN REGARD TO TITHING?

During Jesus' ministry here on earth the Pharisees were the strictest of all the religious sects. They observed all the outward ceremonies and commandments; however, Jesus rebuked them because they were not so careful in regard to what took place on the inside. Matthew 23:23 "For ye pay tithe of mint and anise and cummin, and have omitted the weightier matters of the law — judgment, mercy and faith; these ought ye to have done and not to leave the

Those slow to plant,
will be slow to harvest.

other undone." In Luke 11:42 Jesus said almost the same words to Simon the Pharisee, as He spoke here in Matthew. Both times Jesus said, "These ought ye to have done." It is very important that we note that the only thing that Jesus ever commended in the lives of the scribes and Pharisees was the fact that they were tithers. Yet Jesus said in Matthew 5:20 "That except your righteousness shall exceed the righteousness of the scribes and Pharisees, ye shall in no case enter into the kingdom of heaven." A Pharisee was not only required to tithe, but gave from one-fourth to one-third of his income. It is also important to note that the Pharisees were continually looking for something they could accuse Jesus of. But never once did they ever accuse Him of not tithing.

In Matthew 22:15 The Pharisees came to Jesus regarding the paying of taxes and the paying of tithe. They knew that God required that they should pay their tithe into the temple for the priesthood. But they asked Jesus, because the taxes were so high which they had to pay to Caesar, wouldn't that take the place of their tithe to the Temple? Jesus said: "Render therefore unto Caesar the things which are Caesar's; and unto God the things that are God's." The question is, "What are the things that belong unto God?" "The tithe is the Lord's, it is wholly the Lord's." Jesus endorsed tithing as our debt. The tithe does not belong to us, even as stewards. "It is wholly the Lord's." Jesus did not do away with tithing, but considered it the minimum for Christian giving. He endorsed in the New Testament that we should give liberally over, above, and beyond our tithe. Luke 12:34, Luke 6:38, Luke 21:3 & 4, Acts 20:35.

17. DOES JESUS PRAISE ANYONE FOR TITHING?

When someone makes a payment on what he owes you, you do not praise him because he has not done you any favor. He has just fulfilled his obligation. Jesus made this clear in Matthew 23:23 when He said "For ye pay tithe," not give the tithe. This shows that the tithe is a debt or God's claim on our stewardship.

When we feel we have a right to use our tithe according to our own judgements, we forfeit our stewardship. The tithe is the Lord's, and we have no right to do with it what we please.

The more you put in,
the more you'll get out.

18. IF JESUS FULFILLED THE LAW, THEN WHY SHOULD I TITHE?

When Jesus came and shed His blood for our sins we no longer have to make a blood sacrifice, because by the shedding of His own blood He paid the supreme sacrifice once and for all, for all mankind. We are no longer in bondage to the law because Christ's death set us free. The law never caused man to sin, but rather showed him his sin and shortcomings.

The law is a type of the Roman pedagogue, who did not teach, but was the slave whose duty it was to take the child to the school (*Galatians 3:14 & 25*). The law never made the Jews tithe but rather showed them that they fell short of God's expectation. God's Word shows us that the tithe is a means to let us acknowledge God's ownership (*Leviticus 27:30*).

If tithing is legalistic, then why did Abraham and Jacob tithe a tenth of all they had to God? In their day THERE WAS NO LAW given for at least 500 years later to Moses. The tithe could NOT be a part of the law as it was not given under the law, only practiced under the law as one of God's laws of righteousness.

19. IF TITHING IS NOT A FINANCIAL PROBLEM, WHAT KIND IS IT?

It is a SPIRITUAL problem. One out of every sixty verses in the New Testament deals with stewardship. Money is mentioned six times more than baptism and sixty times more than the Lord's supper. The term "virgin birth" is mentioned only two times, "missions" ten times, while the word "tithing" is used twenty-two times, excluding the words "offerings" and "giving." God has given us direction in Joshua 1:17, in regards to prosperity. His requirements are to meditate in His word, and do what is written therein: *"For then thou shalt make thy way prosperous, and then shalt thou have good success."* The word "good success" in the Hebrew means *"That you will be able to deal wisely in the affairs of life."* It is not only God's will for us to prosper wherever we are, but the promise for our prosperity is dependent upon our meeting the conditions.

20. IF I DON'T TITHE, HOW WILL IT AFFECT MY CHURCH?

Two ways, spiritually and physically. The church is a corporate body; if one is out of step with God's program the whole body will suffer because God said, they are under the curse (*Malachi 3:9*). They can only be blessed by God when they are being obedient and functioning as a corporate body.

21. IS TITHING FOR THE NEW TESTAMENT AGE?

This question would have failed to have any significance in the Early Church — the reason being, "the people sold all they had and brought it to the apostles' feet!" They gave all. During those days they had a communal style of living, and had all things in common. As the church age progressed, this method was found impractical, for people live better in families, than in communes. However, the early church was in an emergency situation because the new christians lived in danger of losing their lives from the continuous persecution by the Jewish leaders. The Christians were glad to live together — to enjoy the mutual security this helped to provide. When the time came that circumstances changed, they moved into their own homes and the communal system of housing was abandoned. This is the reason that tithing was not practiced during the first years of the Early church, because as long as they practiced communal living they gave all they had to the church.

The early church was aware of the fact that communal living was not permanent, so they plainly taught that tithing was also God's plan during the New Testament age. It is true that tithing in the New Testament should be considered a privilege rather than a command. Believers should do things because they love the Lord — not because they are forced to do them. Nevertheless, God's laws concerning prosperity are just as relevant in the New Testament as in the Old.

The book of Hebrews was written some thirty five years after the origin of the New Testament church. *Hebrews 7:8* tells us, *"the Jewish priest though mortal, receives tithes: but we are told that Melchizedek lives on". (Living Bible)* Christ himself is spoken of receiving tithes. Since Jesus is "a priest forever after the order of Melchizedek", and since Abraham is the father of us all through faith, the same principles that led Abraham to pay tithes to Melchizedek, who was the type of Christ, should also lead every member of the body of Christ to honor Christ with his tithes and offerings. To some it may seem when they bring their tithes and offerings to God's house that they are giving it to man. This is not true. Instead, their tithes are being required by Christ Himself. Acting in His high priesthood after the order of Melchizedek, He received tithes from men. And He still does!

Faith Giving will increase your Living

22. WAS TITHING PRACTICED BY THE NEW TESTAMENT CHURCH?

Paul gave very clear directions in I Corinthians 16:2. "Upon the first day of the week let every one of you lay by him in store, as God hath prospered him that there be no gatherings when I come." Also Paul says God has ordained it in I Corinthians 9:14 "They that preach the gospel should live of the gospel." The reason Paul or Jesus did not elaborate on tithing is that the early church was faithfully keeping the law of the Holy Day and the law of the tithe. It was also practiced by the early church fathers, such as, Justin Martyr, Renaeus, Tertullian, Cyprian, and many others, 110-165 A.D., showing that the church of that day followed the apostolic pattern in sharing all their possessions far above their tithe. Irenaius 120-202 A.D. said, "the rule of the perfect life is the same in each Testament." Ambrose 340-397 A.D., "God has received a tenth part for Himself, and therefore it is not lawful for a man to retain what God has reserved for Himself." Augustine 354-430 A.D., "Our ancestors used to abound in wealth of every kind for this reason that they used to give tithes and pay the tax to Caesar . . . we have been unwilling to share the tithe with God, now the whole is taken away." The Scribes and Pharisees gave tithes for whom Christ had not yet shed His blood . . . How can I keep back when He who died for us said, "Except your righteousness shall exceed the righteousness of the Scribes and Pharisees, ye shall in no case enter the Kingdom of Heaven." They gave a tenth. What about you?

23. AS A NEW TESTAMENT CHRISTIAN, HAVE WE BEEN "LIBERATED" FROM THE PRACTICE OF TITHING?

Liberation is often used by some, as an excuse for disobedience or neglect in the name of a new found freedom. We forget that some things don't change when liberty comes. Basically those things that are unchangeable are the principles of God's word. They are established, and His word is changeless. The extension of our understanding of a truth does not in any way alter it. Matthew 5:17 "Think not that I am come to destroy the law, or the prophets: I am not come to destroy, but to fulfill" Jesus came to fulfill the law or to fill

Giving opens the door to God's bank.

the law up. He was not a law breaker, He was a law keeper. The basic thing that Jesus did when He came, was not to destroy or abolish the law but to extend it so it would function in the lives of His people. For example: If you hate someone — you are guilty of the commandment "Thou shalt not kill." Hatred is murder as far as God is concerned. If the eyes of a man or a woman looks on another to the place of desiring an adulterous relationship, then Jesus said: Matthew 5:28 that in the eyes of God adultery has already been performed. As Jesus took the commandments and extended them further, likewise He took the Old Testament principles of giving and did not abolish them but rather perfected and extended them also.

24. IS THERE A DIFFERENCE BETWEEN LEGALISTIC PERFORMANCE AND THAT OF LOVING OBEDIENCE?

This is the principle of the New Testament teaching. We do not bring our tithes and offerings out of a spirit of condemnation, but rather out of a spirit of liberty and love. God's basic giving starts with the tithe. The last verses of the book of Leviticus 27 tells us "The tithe is holy unto the Lord" "The tenth is holy unto the Lord." To be sure there could never be any misunderstanding, the Lord made clear that that which was to be given to Him was the first fruits, not what they had left. There is nothing in the New Testament that even suggests that this principle has been done away with, but rather there is much teaching in the New Testament to show that Jesus and the early church adhered to these principles and guidelines for living. Jesus extends the Ten Commandments in the New Testament too. Matthew 22:37 "Thou shalt love the Lord thy God with all thy heart, and with all thy soul and with all thy mind." In this scripture Jesus is stating that all that we are, and all we have, becomes His. In the Old Testament God wrote his laws on rocks, because of the hardness of men's hearts like stone. But in Jeremiah 31:33 He said the time has come when He would write His law on the fleshly tables of our hearts. When Jesus said, "He came to fulfill the Law" What He was saying was, that He not only lived it in His own life, but He came that His transforming power would so operate in our lives that we would no longer walk after the flesh but after the Spirit.

Giving began with God.
Giving will give you a new direction in ministry.

25. HOW IS GOD'S WISDOM DISPLAYED IN OUR TITHING?

God's wisdom is apparent in many ways. God has seen fit to make His work dependent upon us, and in doing so, we honor Him and acknowledge His ownership. Why did God choose to finance His word through us? Because He knew if he was ever going to make man like himself, he must first teach him to give. If you want God to give you something, you must practice doing what He does — He gives. It would not be hard for one who created all the silver and the gold, and knows where it is deposited throughout the earth, to support His own program. Instead, He used a plan which involves His children by bringing them into partnership with Him. In II Corinthians 8:8 Paul throws out a challenge to Christians by saying, "Prove the sincerity of your love". Giving money to Christ is more than lip service. Since mankind loves money and the things it will buy more than anything else, except his own life — he has no surer way of proving his love than giving it to his Lord. For what we grasp — we lose, and what we surrender — we keep.

26. WHAT IS THE NEW TESTAMENT PLAN FOR THE SUPPORT OF THE CHURCH?

Tithing was known and practiced before there was a Jew, a Levite, or even before there was a Jewish Nation. Tithing is a very important part of Christianity. To be a Christian is to put God first and foremost. To be a tither is to put God first. If one refuses to accept the Lord's teaching in the law of giving, and instead makes a law for himself in regard to giving, it is nothing short of disobedience and rebellion, showing he has chosen to live a life of selfishness rather than self-denial.

Jesus is the founder of the Christian church, and He instituted and ordained the practice of paying tithe for the support of the preaching of the gospel. Paul writes in II Corinthians 9:7-11 regarding the ministry and its maintenance. Also in I Corinthians 9:13 "Do you not know that they which minister about holy things live of the things of the temple? and they which wait at the altar are partakers with the altar?" Paul is reminding them that the priests received their support and living of the things of the temple. That is, of the tithes and offerings that were brought in from the people of God.

Faith is the empty hand of the soul
that reaches out to God and returns full.

And then in *I Corinthians 9:14* "*In the same way, the Lord has given orders that those who preach the Gospel should be supported by those who accept it.*" *(Living Bible)*

Jesus the founder of the christian church endorsed tithing when He said in Matthew 23:23 *(Living Bible)* "*Yes, woe upon you, Pharisees, and you other religious leaders — hypocrites! For you tithe down to the last mint in your garden, but ignore the important things — justice and mercy and faith. Yes, you should tithe, but you shouldn't leave the more important things undone*". After such a statement by Jesus, surely there should never be any question in regard to His putting his approval on it once and for all.

27. SHOULD TITHING BE A TEST OF CHURCH MEMBERSHIP?

Let us phrase the question this way. Should all members agree to tithe when they join the church? Why should there be any objection to doing what is right, especially when Jesus said: Luke 11:42 "These ought ye to have done." We have no right to join anything that we are not willing to support. On the other hand, just because we are not a church member, does not free us from the obligation of paying our tithes and giving our offerings.

Tithing is greater than church membership. It is important to our membership in the body of Christ. If we love Him, we will keep His commandments.

28. SHOULD ALL OF OUR GIVING BE TO THE CHURCH?

No. When we bring "Ye all the tithes" into the church we do not give them, but pay them. Our offerings (not tithes) not only go into the church (but as alms) to be given to help others or to help other ministries. Acts 20:35, "And to remember the words of the Lord Jesus, how He said: it is more blessed to give than to receive." When we give to those in need He promises to give to us also. *Proverbs 19:17 - (Living Bible)* "*When you help the poor you are lending to the Lord, and He pays wonderful interest on your loan.*" Psalms 112:9, 41:1, Proverbs 11:17, 28:27.   We are to be givers not withholders. It is the giver who loves God more than self.

What you give accumulates. God keeps books.
He's never in the red!

29. IF I AM ONE OF THE LARGER TITHERS IN THE CHURCH, SHOULD I HAVE MORE TO SAY IN REGARD TO SPENDING ITS FINANCES?

No. Because the scripture tells us Luke 12:48 "To whom much is given much is required." You have not paid any more than the man who had little tithe, if you both paid in proportion to your income. In fact, it may have been a greater sacrifice for the one with the small salary than the one with the larger salary. Only one person did Jesus ever praise for tithing, and that was the poor widow, because she didn't just pay her tithe but gave her all. (It was only a mite.)

30. WOULD TITHING OF ALL THE MEMBERS SOLVE THE CHURCH'S FINANCIAL PROBLEM?

It is very doubtful if tithing alone would support the whole church program; local, district, and general. But tithes and offerings would, if the offerings were as generous as God laid upon their hearts to give. Faithful tithers who have experienced the joy they have received from tithing will want to know the fulness of joy that comes from giving.

31. WHAT DOES THE BRINGING OF OUR TITHES .AND OFFERINGS DO FOR THE CHURCH?

In Hezekiah's time tithing brought about a revival. Especially II Chronicles 31:5-10 tells about the revival that was held by Hezekiah. God moved on their hearts till the people brought their tithes and offerings to the temple and laid them in heaps, and when this was done, there was plenty to carry on God's work.

32. DOES THE CHURCH NEED MONEY?

Not if God's people are being obedient to God's instruction. Can you imagine God not making provision in His program for the building where He commands His people not to forsake the assembling of themselves together? This is the place they will gather together to pray, praise, worship and learn of Him. God has a program and His program works. If all Christiandom tithed, God's program would never be hampered because of a lack of funds. Paul says in I Corinthians 9:14 God has ordained "They that preach the

The love of money is the root of all evil,
not the *possession of money*.

Gospel should live of the Gospel." As long as we are living in a material world, God's work cannot be carried on without material means.

33. IS IT NECESSARY FOR MEMBERS OF A LOCAL CHURCH TO BRING THEIR TITHES INTO THEIR OWN CHURCH TREASURY?

When one finds a church or body of believers that they choose to commit themselves to in fellowship, it involves their finances. Where your money is, that is where your heart is. Malachi 3:10 tells us to "Bring ye all the tithes into the storehouse." The tithe should go into the church, and the pastor, along with the church council, board, or elders should determine how it should be handled. It is strange how some people are willing to trust their souls to their leaders, but not their money. The New Testament example is so remote from today's practice, that it is difficult at times to compare it with the church today. In the early church there was only one church in each city. Can you imagine the believers sending offerings to areas not sanctioned by the local shepherds? If there is a need in your home, of sickness, juvenile delinquency, drunken husband, divorce, or even death — who do you call? . . . the minister that lives hundreds or even thousands of miles away that is ministering to the multitudes? No. You call the local Pastor that loves you, prays for you, and is always there in a time of need.

34. WOULDN'T VOLUNTARY GIVING BE MORE ACCEPTABLE TO MAN THAN TITHES AND OFFERINGS?

It may be more acceptable but not more practical. Because then man would only be giving by impulse, and the church could not be properly supported by voluntary giving any more than our country could. Suppose all taxes were abolished, and tax collectors were sent out to the people to appeal to their patriotism, by taking up a free will offering. We would become the laughing stock of the nations of the world.

If this is foolish in the natural, how do we think God feels about this indifferent, hit-or-miss give-when-you-can, or when you-feel-like-it, method of supporting His church which His Son gave His life for. I'm sure it must be an insult to His intelligence.

Miracles don't come out of the blue,
God sends them.

35. WHY DOES THE CHURCH ALWAYS LACK MONEY?

Because man is no longer following God's pattern. Our Father never left one thing undone, and above all the things He made provision for was the upkeep of His House. If the church is ever in need, or the doors are ever closed, it is not the result of God's failure, but of man's disobedience to the plan and commandments of God to bring his tithes and offerings into the storehouse.

36. CAN I GIVE PART OF MY TITHE TO HELP SUPPORT RELATIVES, OR A CHARITY ORGANIZATION?

No. The scripture tells us in Malachi 3:10 that "All" the tithe is to be brought into the storehouse for the support of the ministry. The Mosiac Law made provision for the poor in Leviticus 19:9-10, and Deuteronomy 24:19-21. Further illustrations of this principle are found in Ruth 2:15 & 16. This same principle has been incorporated in our New Testament laws. After the tithe, then I John 3:17-18 tells us we are to give offerings for the poor. Jesus summed it all up when He said these words in Matthew 25:34-46 (Verse 40) "In-as-much as ye have done it unto one of the least of these my brethren, ye have done it unto me."

37. WHY DOESN'T THE CHURCH TAKE CARE OF ALL THE POOR?

So many ask why there are so many charities doing the work of the church in taking care of the poor. The reason — there are no finances to take care of them. People today grumble because God requires one-tenth, but our giving doesn't even compare with the giving in Bible days. Their first tithe was the support of the Priest and Levites. When they had national feasts, they brought in a second tithe, and they were to bring in twelve different offerings. Then every third year they were required to pay a third tithe to take care of the poor. That is why the early church was able to care for the poor, when the church today is not. But is it possible for us who are under grace not to exceed those that were under law, when we enjoy so many blessings of God that they did not?

If we are to know the joy of receiving,
we must first know the joy of giving.

38. SHOULD THE POOR BE ENCOURAGED TO GIVE?

Jesus used for an example the widow with only two mites, Luke 21:1-4. He took the opportunity to show that He honored and encouraged giving — even by the poorest person. God is not impressed by the size of the gift, but by the spirit of the giver. To the natural mind it seems that Jesus would have admonished her to keep her little offering to meet her own needs, especially when there were rich men casting large sums into the treasury. But Jesus never stopped her, instead He commended what she did, in fact He had her act recorded so it would be an example to all men in the ages to come. Her end must have been like that of the poor widow in I Kings 17:8-16 who gave her last cake to Elijah the man of God, instead of keeping it for her son and herself. Because of this act of faith "the barrel of meal wasted not, neither the cruse of oil fail".

One great mistake that is often made on the mission field or in poor areas is that the people are allowed to believe that they are too poor to pay their tithe or to give. This kind of thinking and teaching will rob them of the blessings God has for them. God encourages the poor to give, for it is only in their giving that they will find financial liberation and can have the assurance that God will supply all their needs.

39. WHO PROMISED TO PAY US BACK IF WE GIVE TO THOSE IN NEED?

Proverbs 19:17 "He that hath pity upon the poor lendeth unto the Lord; and that which he hath given will He pay him again." *(Living Bible)* "He pays wonderful interest on your loan."   Psalms 41:1 "Blessed is he that considereth the poor; the Lord will deliver him in his time of trouble." II Corinthians 9:13 (Phillips) "Moreover, your very giving proves the reality of your faith, and that means that men thank God that you practice the gospel of Christ that you profess to believe in, as well as for the actual gifts your fellowship makes to them and to others."

Facts will put you in bondage,
while faith will open doors
of blessing.

Part IV

1. WHAT IS THE SPIRITUAL SIDE OF TITHING?

We lay so much stress on the financial blessing the tither is going to get, that we often neglect the spiritual blessing which is far more important. When we tithe, we have the assurance and satisfaction of knowing we are putting God first in our lives and that we are actually in partnership with God — an all-knowing, all-powerful God who can bring to pass those things that are best for us spiritually, as well as physically and financially. The tither has real joy in realizing that he is God's partner too and that he is having a part in advancing God's program in the world today. Tithing is not only a financial plan, but a scriptural plan, and the only financial plan that is suggested in the word of God. When God's tithing system is not used, then the church has to resort to man-made methods of raising money that in the end are spiritually deadening. The Lord loveth a cheerful giver — a giver who shares his material benefits because he loves the cause of Christ. The system of Tithes and offerings is not merely a duty, but a spiritual act — an act of worship which brings a spiritual blessing. The tithe is not given to men, but to God — the blessing promised is from Him.

2. IS TITHING, IN ANY WAY RESPONSIBLE TO CHRISTIAN GROWTH?

Tithing is indeed a source of Christian growth and joy. The spontaneous giver who refuses to give systematically almost always gives in spurts, and gives less than those who give faithfully what God has required. Disobedience can be caused by lack of faith in God's faithfulness, that He will do what He says. Liberality means sowing and reaping when people discover that God's financial principle not only pays them financially, but also frees the spirit from materialistic death. Proverbs 11:25 "The liberal soul shall be made fat." One who believes this, will not just stop at tithing. II Corinthians 9:6 & 11.

Tithing, a Scriptural principle:
Commanded in the Old Testament,
commended in the New.

3. IF I ONLY WORK PART TIME, AND MY SALARY WILL NOT SUPPORT MY FAMILY, SHOULD I TITHE?

God never makes any exception in any of His commandments or with any of His promises. The greater our need is, the greater opportunity we have to "Prove me now herewith." No matter how small your income, when you have paid God, the rest will go a lot farther. Matthew 6:24-34 tells us not to be anxious, that God will take care of us.

4. SHOULD SOMEONE TITHE WHILE IN DEBT?

Yes, if you want to get out of debt. The natural man says, no. Proverbs 14:12, "There is a way that seemeth right unto man, but the end thereof are the ways of death." We forget we owed God a long time before we owed these debts. He rightfully has first claim. Matthew 6:33 promises that if we will put Him first, all these other things will be added unto us, and in this way every need will be met. Why should we tithe while in debt? Because we must also remember that we are in partnership, and we are handling the money that belongs to our silent partner, and it requires that He gets His rightful part off the top. If He does not get it, then it is called embezzlement. It is important to pay Him His part, for He is looking out for our interests and can enable us to go deeper into debt or to prosper so we might get out of debt.

5. IF WE SAY EVERYTHING WE HAVE IS THE LORD'S, THEN WHY DO WE SAY ONE-TENTH IS THE LORD'S?

The word "tithe" means one-tenth. The very fact that the scriptures prescribe offerings above our tithe proves that the tithe is the minimum that God requires. If we prove faithful in the little things, God will bless us with many things as He did the servants He entrusted the talents to.

6. SHOULD WE PAY TITHE BEFORE DEDUCTING OUR CURRENT EXPENSES?

Yes. Take the tithe out first, then budget the rest to meet the needs. Sometimes this seems impossible when we have large families and small incomes, but He still promises in Matthew 6:33 "Seek ye

God will give more back to us,
so we can give more back to Him.

42

first the kingdom of God and His righteousness and all these things (temporal things) will be added unto you."

7. CAN I DEDUCT SOCIAL SECURITY AND INCOME TAX BEFORE PAYING MY TITHE?

No. Because we tithe on our gross and not our net.
When we try to see how little we can get by with, it shows that we have not seen the spiritual principle of giving.

Systematic giving shows where our dependence is, and God in turn provides in more ways than we could ever dream of.

8. AFTER I TITHE, AM I RESPONSIBLE FOR WHAT IS LEFT?

Yes. As good stewards, .it is every believer's responsibility to manage his household well. In this day of credit cards and payment plans, every child of God must beware of getting caught up in the whirlpool of materialism, interest rates and go-now-pay-later plans! If you would ask a four year old, "Do you want fifty cents now or five dollars tomorrow? We know their answer would be "I want it now". The child of God should exhibit a maturity.

9. SHOULD GIFTS RECEIVED BY LEGACIES BE TITHED?

If we must tithe from that which we've earned, most assuredly the gifts that cost us nothing should be tithed.

10. HOW CAN ONE TITHE WITHOUT ANY CERTAIN INCOME?

If there is no definite income, then you tithe whatever comes into your hands.

11. IF I AM BUYING MY HOME, WHY CAN'T I DEDUCT MY PAYMENTS BEFORE TITHING?

Because the money that you invested in your home would bring an income if it had been otherwise invested. Therefore, it must be included in living of the family. If you have several rented homes, you can deduct taxes and upkeep but not the interest, for the rent becomes the interest on the investment. Just one word of wisdom. The more liberal you are with God, the more liberal He will be with you.

Planting a bigger field means
reaping a bigger harvest.

12. WHAT IS THE DIFFERENCE BETWEEN TITHING THE INCOME AND THE INCREASE?

Our income is what we receive from labor, or investments. Our increase is the increase of our investment. In other words, if you buy a home and pay $95,000 for it and in a few years, sell it for $110,000, you would tithe on the $15,000 profit. If you buy a car for $5,000 and sell it for $5,200, you would again tithe on the $200 profit. The same example would apply to bonds. If you invested $1,000 and at the end of ten years you would receive $2,000, you would tithe on the $1,000; of course, with the thought in mind that the principal had been tithed on previously.

13. WHAT IS THE NET INCOME?

A person who works and receives regular wages should have no trouble in determining his net income, as all his income as a rule is net and should be tithed. If his wages are $200.00 a week, his tithe would be $20.00. The only time deductions are possible are in the case of a doctor or someone like him who used his car solely for his practice. He may deduct the overhead. Or a farmer could deduct the cost of seed purchased, fertilizer, outside help that has been hired in the raising and harvesting of the crop, but the living of the farmer's family would not be a deductible expense.

It is a fact that many tithers gladly tithe of their gross income without deducting any expenses. The reason they do is because they have found out a very important secret. That is, you can't outgive God, and the Lord loves a loyal tither and a cheerful giver.

14. DO I TITHE ON MY GROSS EARNINGS OR MY TAKE-HOME PAY?

This answer is easily determined. What does the government tax you on? Your gross income of course, because that is what you earned or they would not have been able to deduct insurance, social security, etc. These deductions are made primarily for your benefit from your earnings. How you figure your tithe will determine your motive and your faith. We should not give according to our income or circumstances, but we should give according to our motive.

15. IS TITHING COMPULSORY?

No. Nothing in Christianity is compulsory. Jesus didn't have to come to this world and die for us. He came because He loved us and knew if He did not come, we would be eternally lost. He doesn't make us follow Him, but He extends an invitation to us and we can either accept Him, or reject Him and be eternally lost. If you want to be a disciple of Christ and keep His commandments, that is your choice.

If you have been giving God the leftovers of your income instead of His tithe then you have been depriving yourself of one of the greatest joys in your Christian life. You have been cutting yourself off from the blessings, both spiritual and financial, that come from partnership with God. The effectiveness of our witness is determined both by the way we make our money and how we spend it, and how much of it we give to God. For when a man does not know the true nature of the things he possesses, he does not possess them, they possess him. Because a man's intellect may be expanded by ideas, but the heart can only be expanded by love.

Why did God ordain tithing? Was it to place an increased burden and taxation upon us? Don't let us misunderstand God's love and wisdom! It isn't that God needs our tithe. He could have established a different system for carrying out His Work. But to have done so would have robbed us of the blessing that flows back to us if we are faithful in tithes and offerings. For the tithe is not only a debt we owe, but also a seed we sow.

TITHING AS A CHRISTIAN DUTY

Abraham commanded it	Genesis 14:18-20
Jacob continued it	Genesis 28:22
Moses confirmed it	Leviticus 27:30-33
Malachi commanded it	Malachi 3:8-10
Christ commended it	Matthew 23:23
Believers profit by it	Malachi 3:11
God's work is advanced by it	I Cor. 16:2
God's people are blessed by it	Malachi 3:10

Expecting a return is not sacrilegious;
this is doing business with God.

45

Part V

1. WHAT IS THE DIFFERENCE BETWEEN TITHES AND OFFERINGS?

The difference is that our tithes we pay God, and our offerings we give to God. Matthew 23:23, Jesus said to the Pharisees "For ye pay tithe." Many have said God never blesses me so I can give Him above my tithe. The reason God has not blessed you sufficiently is because you have tried to turn God's word around to suit yourself. In every promise of the Bible there is a condition and God always requires us to make the first move. he tells us in *Luke 6:38 "Give and it shall be given unto you."* This is not tithe, it is an offering because He is encouraging us to learn the secret of giving. David said he gave over and above. *(I Chronicles 29:3.)*

2. DID GOD CHARGE THAT WE ROBBED HIM IN TITHES ONLY?

No. In tithes and offerings. So many today stop with the word tithes, for they wouldn't think of not paying them. But what about a regular offering? We take time to pray and ask God to lead us and guide us, but do we take time to ask Him what to give? The word "and" is a conjunction connecting the words tithes and offerings together, and who are we to try to separate them. His blessing is promised for those that bring in their tithes and offerings — not just one or the other. The tithe is a debt or tax we pay, but an offering is a gift of love above our tithe which, when we bring it, will open the windows of heaven. Dr. Pacock explains it "I will pour out on you such a blessing as shall not be enough only, and such as shall be sufficient, but more and more than enough."

When God sent a pestilence upon the children of Israel because they had sinned, David prayed to the Lord in their behalf confessing his sin, and God sent the prophet Gad to David and told him to go to the threshing floor of Araunah and build an altar to offer up a sacrifice. David obeyed the Lord and when he offered to buy it Araunah told him he would give it to him. David said: II Samuel 24:24, "Nay: but I will surely buy it of thee at a price:

Money is not evil. It is an instrument
for carrying out God's work.

46

neither will I offer burnt sacrifices unto the Lord my God of that which doth cost me nothing." Our apostleship costs us nothing, but our discipleship costs us everything.

3. HOW MUCH OFFERING SHOULD WE GIVE?

God leaves that up to you. Deuteronomy 8:17 & 18. It seems there are so many Christians who try to figure what they can deduct, so they won't have to pay as much tithe or offering. But God has an answer for that. Luke 6:38 'Give and it shall be given unto you; good measure, pressed down, and shaken together, and running over, shall men give into your bosom. For with the same measure that ye mete withal it shall be measured to you again." II Corinthians 9:6 & 7 "But this I say, He which soweth sparingly shall reap also sparingly; and he which soweth bountifully shall reap also bountifully. Every man according as he purposeth in his heart, so let him give; not grudgingly, or of necessity: for God loveth a cheerful giver." God doesn't want your tithe or offering just out of duty, but He wants it with joy because you love Him and want to share with Him the blessings He has bestowed upon you. Some say, "No one ever gives me anything." May I ask the question, "How much do you give God?" It will come back with the same measure, only God's measure seems to be bigger when He gives back. The more you cut down on God, the more He will cut down on you. God blessed Israel because they offered willingly. *(I Chronicles 29:6, 9 & 17.)*

4. TO WHAT EXTENT DOES GOD EXPECT ME TO GIVE?

Giving to God, is what the world calls a foolish thing. When God asks for a portion of our money, He not only feels, but knows He has a right to it, because He knows that if it wasn't for Him we would not have anything. On the basis of this fact, God is saying: I expect the starting point from you in showing your allegiance to me. Paul, in speaking of the church of Macedonia uses them as an example in II Corinthians 8:1-5, that they gave while they were in deep poverty and in great trial of affliction, and gave beyond their own power. He goes on to say in Verse 5, that the reason they were able to do this was because they first gave themselves unto the Lord. As a result their deep poverty and affliction abounded unto an abundance of joy that money cannot buy or the world cannot take away.

"Seek ye the kingdom of God; and all these
things shall be added unto you."

5. WHY IS IT SO HARD FOR SOME PEOPLE TO PART WITH THEIR TITHES AND OFFERINGS?

Because they have forgotten to Whom it belongs. We say — My money, My tithe, My offering. Jesus gave us an illustration of this when He told about the man that God had blessed and prospered. No doubt he had worked hard and made good investments — *Luke 12:15, 20 and 21.* Then he forgot God and said: My fruits, My barns, My goods. God said: *"Thou fool, this night thy soul shall be required of thee" (Luke 12:20).* If his soul belonged to him, how could God require it? If it was his money and his property, why couldn't he take it with him? We can't take anything with us when we die. In fact we can't even be sure of it while we are alive, for sudden reverses can come and wipe it all away. This is why Jesus went on to say . . . *"Then whose shall these things be which thou hast provided?" (Verse 20).* *"So is he that layeth up treasure for himself, and is not rich toward God".* (Verse 21).

Here is an example of a man who violated God's principles and lost his life. —   Luke 12:17-20
1. He made no provision for abundance — (12:17).
2. He spent his wealth on himself and his own program.
3. He confused material goods with security — (12:20).
4. He made no provision for his goods after death — (12:20).

5 Keys to Abundance. —   Luke 12:22-36
1. Have a true estimate of life, (12:22)
2. Believe God wants to take care of you, (12:24-30)
3. Pursue the principles of kingdom living, (12:31)
4. Have faith, He will supply your needs, (12:32)
5. Transfer your goods into ministering currency, (12:33, 34).

6. WHY IS EVERYONE TODAY LOOKING FOR SECURITY?

There is — Social Security, life insurance, hospital insurance, retirement insurance, etc. Nowadays it is necessary to have these things to live in our society. In most insurances you are promised double dividends in case of accidental death. The ironic thing about this is, if necessary we let other things go in order to pay it. However, when we die we don't collect it,

Giving your firstfruits is like a good farmer planting his best seed in the earth.

someone else does. God's insurance is the only insurance that we can collect after death. That is, when we bring our tithes and offerings to God's House, we will not only have the assurance of His blessing here, but at the same time we will be laying treasures up there.

But remember you cannot lay treasures up there until you first are willing to lay them down here. Satan not only wants the money we made last week, but he also wants to tie up the money we will be making for the next five or ten years. He keeps trying to get us to stick our necks into his yoke, so we will get ourselves into such financial bondage that if God should speak to us to give, we would not be able to do so. Satan does not want us to be in a position to be obedient to God, for in doing so it would put us in a position to receive the blessings that God has for us. The battle of giving is over when we recognize that all we have belongs to God, and that He has just made us His trustees.

7. WHY HAS THE JOY GONE OUT OF TAKING OFFERINGS IN THE CHURCH?

Because we have forgotten that it is as much a part of our worship to the Lord as the singing of a hymn or the praying of a prayer. It is the fruit of our labor that we are bringing to worship Him with. Offering plates have been instituted by man to take the offering as quickly as possible to keep the service within the limited time, and as a result we have lost the joy we should have when we bring our tithes and offerings to worship Him.

8. WHY MUST OUR GIVING BE ACCOMPLISHED THROUGH LOVE?

I Corinthians 13:3 "And have not charity (love) it profiteth me nothing." Love knows no boundaries. When love motivates our giving, we do it with joy. God wants His people to see that giving and receiving money is a flowing interchange between our act of faith and His unlimited resources, and is based on His immutable law of sowing and reaping. New Testament giving, is to give out of the bounty of God toward us, instead of giving out of requirements placed on us.

If you don't like Old Testament tithing,
then take New Testament giving. "Give all."

49

It helps us to overcome covetousness, self, and the flesh. In giving our money it makes us heaven-conscious, and gives us a love for men and for God's work. Luke 12:34. How different are our standards than Christ's? When it comes to giving, the world asks, what does a man owe? Jesus asks, how does he use it? The world asks how much did he keep? We look at the gift. Jesus asks whether or not the gift was a sacrifice. Tithing is only an Old Testament principle in the sense that when they had discharged their duty, they didn't have to do anything else. While in the New Testament we have to be willing to love too, and go beyond duty, to where love flows. Tithing is based on our faithfulness to the word of God so that we might be partakers of God's benefits. Jesus said in John 14:21 "He that hath my commandments, and keepeth them, he it is that loveth me: and he that loveth me shall be loved of my Father, and I will love him, and will manifest myself to him."

The rule of the believer's life is gracious — not legal. The justified believer is a son in the family of God, not a servant of the law. Therefore our motive is not of having to, but of wanting to out of love.

9. WHY MUST I GIVE IN ORDER TO WORSHIP GOD?

Because it is impossible to worship without giving. When a person sings, prays or praises, it involves giving out of self to the Lord. If a person sits on the side line as a spectator like watching television, he only receives. But to worship, he must be involved by participating. Psalms 29:1 & 2 "Give unto the Lord the glory due unto His name; worship the Lord in the beauty of holiness." Psalms 30:4 "Sing unto the Lord, O ye saints of His, and give thanks". . . . . Psalms 96:8 Give unto the Lord the glory due unto His name; bring an offering, and come into His courts." We can only relate through giving. We pray over our food and say, "Lord we thank you for this food; bless it to our bodies in Jesus name." Giving according to the New Testament is another way of saying, "Thank you, Lord!" Giving is a grace, or thanksgiving to God.

10. WHAT WILL HAPPEN WHEN WE GIVE?

Proverbs 11:24 & 25 "There is that scattereth, and yet increaseth; and there is that withholdeth more than is meet, but it tendeth to poverty." The (Living) Bible expresses it this way: "It is possible to give

"God loveth a cheerful giver."

away and become richer! It is also possible to hold on too tightly and lose everything. Yes, the liberal man shall be rich! By watering others, he waters himself." Can we trust Jesus with it? It is a Biblical principle; You multiply what you give away, and you lose what you keep. This applies at every level of our life — financially, physically, and spiritually. You will lose what you keep, but you will multiply what you give away. There is only one thing you will ever get from God without giving first, and that is salvation — His gift to all mankind. Where we find most satisfaction in life is when we give, because God created us in His image, and God is on the giving hand. We feel most like God, when we do things like God. He gives, gives, and gives. The world says: "Obtain." "Possess." "Acquire." "Hold on to." God says — "Give." "Invest." "Distribute." "Share." Does God pay attention to what we give? He told Cornelius He did. Acts 10:4.

11. WHAT WILL HAPPEN IF WE DON'T GIVE?

We cannot expect to receive, Luke 6:8 "Give and it shall be given unto you." If we don't give we are keeping God's hands tied. Nothing times nothing equals nothing. Also we would be expecting God to break one of His own laws, and this He will not do as He honors His word above His name. It is only when we give our offerings, that we open the purse strings of heaven, so God can give back. By faith we have acted upon His word. Mark 16:20 . . . "Confirming the word with signs following." Giving is the expression of love in action. Moving out of self into the love of God.

12. WHAT DOES OUR LOVE FOR GOD HAVE TO DO WITH OUR GIVING?

The foundation of Christianity is built on love. For God so loved the world that He GAVE. Jesus GAVE His life a ransom for all. Everything we are, everything we have, and everything we hope to be, is dependent upon His giving it to us. Romans 8:32 "He that spared not his own Son, but delivered him up for us all, how shall he not with him also freely give us all things?" James 1:17 "Every good gift and every perfect gift is from above, and cometh down from the Father of lights." I Chronicles 29:14 "All things come of thee, and of thine own have we given thee." Why then, you ask, does He want it back? For the same reason a husband wants love expressed by his

"It is more blessed to give than to receive."

51

wife. It is proof of our love. We can never question His love because He proved it by giving His dearest possession. Are we willing to do the same? When we really love Him, it is no longer a question of how much must I give, but how much can I give? II Corinthians 8:8 & 9 "And to prove the sincerity of your love. For ye know the grace of our Lord Jesus Christ, that, though He was rich, yet for your sakes He became poor, that ye through His poverty might be rich."

13. WHY DOES GOD WANT AND EXPECT ME TO GIVE?

Reaching out to Jesus involves love, and self-giving. You can't reach out to Jesus in genuine love without giving, anymore than a husband can truly love his wife without giving. Giving is the tangible expression of love. You can't separate loving service from giving. God is interested in my every day life. He is concerned about me and the things that concern me — my health and my desire to prosper and to be happy. He doesn't will me bad, but good (Romans 8:28). I express my love to God by what I give right now. By giving I prove Him and His promise every day and He never disappoints me. Acts 20:35. "It is more blessed to give than to receive. Why? Because in giving, you open the way for God to give back to you. "Give, and it shall be given unto you." Notice, Jesus is talking about giving before it is given to you — about something different than tithe, He is talking about a man giving on faith, believing that God is going to restore him manyfold. When we pray over our food, we thank Him and ask Him to bless it to our bodies. Giving according to the New Testament is another way of saying "Thank you, Lord!" Giving is a grace, or thanksgiving to God.

> "What? Giving again"?
> I cried in dismay,
> "And must I keep giving
> and giving away."
>
> "Oh, no" said the angel
> piercing me through.
> "Just give till the Father
> stops giving to you."

Someone said, "I don't like to hear them talk about giving in the

"Whatsoever a man soweth, that shall he also reap."

church. It kills the spirit." If it does, the only spirit it will kill is — the human spirit!

14. SHOULD CHRISTIANS MAKE A WILL?

Should a Christian be a good steward? Jesus said he should, in every area of his life. Wills and legacies are a wonderful way to give to God. It is true that we should remember those we love here on earth (Proverbs 13:22 — *Living Bible)* But our thoughts and love should extend beyond even that. They should extend all the way to His eternal kingdom that knows no end.

It is wonderful to be faithful to God in our lifetime, but why not also be faithful in death. As stewards or trustees, we are to handle God's wealth in such a way that it will give Him glory in life and in death.

15. IS GIVING TO WORLD MISSIONS A PART OF THE TITHE?

NO. Our regular tithes and offerings are to be brought in that there may be meat in His house, for the foreign field can never be any stronger than the home field. It is a sacrificial offering above our regular tithes and offerings, because we have a burden for lost souls. It is then that we lay ourselves open for blessings from God that we will not receive at any other time. In the great commission Jesus gave, He said: Mark 16:15 "Go ye into all the world, and preach the gospel to every creature. He that believeth and is baptized shall be saved; but he that believeth not shall be damned." If we really believe these words of our Master, we will be impelled to do something about it. We can fill our obligation of going, by giving to support those whom God has called and anointed for this ministry. Maybe we cannot be there to see the results of our labor, but in that day the sower and the reaper will go hand in hand rejoicing bringing in the sheaves. I Samuel 24:24,"But as his part is that goeth down to the battle, so shall his part be that tarrieth by the stuff: they shall part alike."

16. IF GOD CHOOSES TO BLESS AND PROSPER ME, DOES HE HAVE ANY REQUIREMENTS ON HOW I AM TO USE THE MONEY?

To those who have learned the blessing of giving liberally to God's program, God continues to increase their ability to give by blessing

Solomon said: "Withholding tendeth to poverty."

them even more. Those whom God has chosen to bless in this manner because of their faithfulness, know that these temporal blessings are not to be used just for personal pleasures or luxurious living. They realize that in this life we are only stewards, and that which has been entrusted into our keeping, is to be used for the advancement of His kingdom. God's word in Proverbs 3:22 endorses laying up some provision for our children. However, we should be careful not to lay up so much wealth for them that they could misuse or squander it to the point that it might even be responsible for their ruination.

It is true that God needs people of means today; those who are able to give largely to the cause of Christ — those who are unimpressed by their wealth and are consecrated to fulfill the purpose of God.

17. WHY DO SOME CHRISTIANS SAY "I DON'T WANT ANY OF THIS WORLD'S GOODS"?

It is because they do not realize who their money belongs to. The good things of this world were made by God — not for the world, but for His children. Satan came and stole it away from them, and cheated them out of that which was rightfully theirs, because they forgot they were heirs of the father who declared: "All the earth is mine and the fulness thereof." Isaiah 1:19 "If ye be willing and obedient, ye shall eat of the good of the land." It is our promise that we can eat well, dress well, and live well.

18. IS IT A SIN TO HAVE GOOD THINGS?

If it were a sin to have riches, then God would be the biggest sinner in the world. If it is a sin to be rich, then God sinned when He caused Abraham to become rich. If it is wrong to prosper, then God sinned when He prospered David (I Chronicles 29:28), and Solomon (II Chronicles 1:11). The devil says that you must not tempt the Lord by relating money to God's blessings. On the other hand, we never let Satan make us forget that our Father created all the gold, silver, minerals, precious stones, forests, rivers, flocks and herds on this earth, and that heaven's streets are paved with pure gold, its gates are of one solid pearl and its foundations are of precious stones. So, if wealth is carnal and evil, our Father created that evil, and heaven is full of it.

When one truly gives himself to the Lord, all other giving becomes easy!

19. DO WE HAVE A RIGHT TO CLAIM GOD'S PROMISES REGARDING MONEY AND EXPECT TO RECEIVE THEM?

Yes. Money is here on earth — not up in heaven. We have the right to tell Satan to take his hands off of our money, because it was created and provided by our Father. Satan's angels can hinder and keep things from us, while God's angels can loose things for us. God honors faith and God is not poor, so anything He promises in His word, He is able to perform. You say, "but some of God's promises were made to Israel." This is true, but Romans 4:11 tells us that we are sons and heirs through Abraham, and the promises made to Abraham also belong to us.

20. IS IT WRONG FOR A CHRISTIAN TO BE RICH?

No. But I Timothy 6:17 charges those that are rich to be careful regarding two things. ". . . *Not to be highminded; nor trust in uncertain riches, but in the living God who giveth us richly all things to enjoy."* There is nothing wrong with riches in themselves, but the danger is that men start trusting in his riches instead of in God and therefore allows the riches to start dictating and directing their lives until money becomes their goal in life.

Note: The scripture does not charge the Christians that are rich to get rid of their riches, but simply, don't trust in them, but in the living God. *(Proverbs 23:4 & 5) (II Timothy 6:7 & 8).*

21. CAN A CHRISTIAN HAVE A BANK ACCOUNT?

God has a financial and economic plan and program for every one of His children. We don't have to wait until we get to Heaven to enjoy all of God's blessings. God tells us if we are making regular deposits in the bank of Heaven, we should also be able to make some withdrawals. *(Matthew 6:21)* clarifies the place where it should be laid up. It also declares who we are laying it up for. "For yourselves." The great thing about the bank of heaven is — that it is not subject to the money market, stock market, or which party is in power. By telling us of a better bank in Heaven He is not saying it is wrong to have a savings or checking account down here. Proverbs 22:19 tells us to be "diligent in business." In our society today we find that a checking and savings account is a very safe and economical way of doing business.

Love and giving could be synonymous
because they both mean the same to God.

55

22. SHOULD A CHRISTIAN INVEST, SAVE OR HOARD FOR THE FUTURE?

INVEST — YES. But it is important for us to remember that it is God who has given us the money to invest and multiply. Also He will only supply that which we are capable of handling. If we are faithful, often times He will give us even more. However, we must remember that wealth can be either creative or corruptive. *(Luke 19:12-24)*

SAVE — YES. We are to be good stewards in every aspect of our lives. *(Proverbs 21:20)*

HOARD — NO. God does not want us to live in poverty, because our security is not to be in money, but in the living God. To hoard means when we die we will leave everything *(Psalms 49:10-12)*. God did not condemn the rich for their wealth in Luke 12:16-20 but because he decided to hoard it and store it away instead of sharing it.

23. WHAT IS GOD'S PROGRAM IN REGARDS TO GIVING?

"Give to Christ . . . through the Church . . . for the World."

GIVE TO CHRIST — You cannot separate finances from the spiritual. It is a mutual love affair. The more you get to know Jesus and receive from Him, the more of yourself and possessions you will want to give back to Him. *"You can give without loving, but you can't love without giving."*

THROUGH THE CHURCH — The church is the place that God is transacting His business here on earth. The church does not belong to us but to God. We acknowledge this fact and call it God's house by bringing God's tithe and our offerings there to worship Him.

THE CHURCH CAN REACH THE WORLD — for Christ, but it takes money. God gave the means to spread the gospel, but instead the world wants to amass and accumulate it. James 5:3 *"Ye have heaped treasure together for the last days."* The great commission is to "GO". Not everyone is called to go, but every one is called to give to support those who are called *(Romans 10:13)*.

*"It is your Father's good pleasure
to give you the kingdom."*

56

24. IS GETTING OUR NEEDS MET CONDITIONAL OR UNCONDITIONAL?

There are those who seem to think that tithing and giving is a choice that has been left up to them, not a requirement that requires specific obedience. They seem to think that Philippians 4:19 is an unconditional promise. *"But my God shall supply all your needs according to His riches in glory by Christ Jesus."* However it is a conditional promise because it begins with the word *"But,"* which links it with the previous thought found in Verse 18. Paul had received a sacrificial gift from the Philippian church. It was on the basis of their generosity that Paul had declared that God would meet all their needs. Note: That this promise was to those who had already given.

25. DOES GOD WANT HIS SERVANTS TO PROSPER?

More than that. He says He has pleasure in it. Psalms 35:27 *"Let them shout for joy and be glad, that favor my righteous cause: yea let them say continually, Let the Lord be magnified, which hath pleasure in the prosperity of His servant.* Psalms 84:11 *"Be anxious for nothing"* or *"No thing."* You don't have to overcome your Father's reluctance, *"For it is your Father's good pleasure to give you the kingdom."* Luke 12:32 God wants His people to prosper, He does not necessarily want them to be rich. *"Labor not to be rich"* Proverbs 23:4&5 However He wants us to prosper in every area of our lives, not only materially but also in our spirit. A rich man is one who operates daily knowing God's resources are available to him. This man is never motivated by money, nor does he live fearing the lack of it, for it is God's greatest desire to release His resources through us as His extensions in this world. It is true that Satan is a robber and a thief but he cannot steal our claim which has been staked on God's promises. *"No good thing will He withhold from them that walk uprightly."* II Corinthians 9:6 *"He which soweth bountifully shall reap also bountifully."* Proverbs 3:9 *"Honour the Lord with thy substance, and with the first fruits of all thine increase. So shall thy barns be filled with plenty, and thy presses shall burst out with new wine."* Proverbs 8:21 *"That I may cause those that love me to inherit substance; and I will fill their treasures."*

*"The blessing of the Lord, it maketh rich
and addeth no sorrow with it." — Proverbs 10:22*

26. IS TITHING THE SOLUTION FOR ALL CHURCH FINANCES?

Yes, but more than that it applies to the individual also. Not everyone that tithes will go to top management of some big company, or to great prosperity. However there are many scriptures that confirm the fact that we cannot outgive God . . . *"And he that soweth bountifully shall also reap bountifully." (II Corinthians 9:6)* . . . *"If I will not open to you the windows of heaven, and pour you out a blessing, that there shall not be room enough to receive it." (Malachi 3:10)* Obviously some will prosper more than others, owing to their gifts or opportunity. But as God is no respecter of persons His promises are for all believers, whether it be more or less than others, it is more than it would have been had we not been faithful in Christian stewardship.

27. IS THERE ONLY ONE PLACE WHERE JESUS ENDORSED TITHING?

Matthew 23:23 is the only place in the Bible (other than it's parallel passage in *Luke 11:42)* where Jesus endorsed tithing. It is important to point out that Jesus only said once *"Ye must be born again"* and that was to Nicodemus. *(John 3:3)* The fact it was only said once does not lessen its truth or importance. *"Ye must be born again"* — must — is a strong term and it is important to point out that the same Greek word used in *John 3:7* is the same word used in *Matthew 23:12 "These ought ye to have done, and not leave the other undone."* The Greek word deo (from which we get our word debt) means obligation or necessity. Jesus made no idle comments. His approval and exhortation to tithe ought to be sufficient motivation for any Christian. The fact that Jesus said it proves that tithing was not a part of the law but was to be a permanent principle. Paul did not mention hell, but Jesus said enough about it so that Paul did not need to. When Paul did allude to it *(Romans 5:9, II Thessalonians 1:9)* it merely cohered with all Jesus said about it. So it was with tithing. Paul was an articulate Jew who knew the Old Testament backward and forward. I am sure he used the word tithe when building up the faith of the saints and they knew exactly what he meant in the phrase *"As God has prospered him." (I Corinthians 16:2) "In keeping with his income" (New International Version)*

28. WHY SHOULD WE GIVE CHEERFULLY?

"And God is able to make all grace abound toward you, that ye, always having all sufficiency in all things, may abound to every good work." II Corinthians 9:8 *"and God is able to make all grace (every favor and earthly blessing) come to you in abundance, so that you may always and all circumstances and whatever the need, be self-sufficient — possessing enough to require no aid or support and furnished in abundance for every good work and charitable donation. (Amplified Translation)* Paul also not only exhorts the Christian to be a cheerful giver because of the promise of blessing, but also a protection against bitterness should God withhold His blessing. If we give cheerfully we will give because it is right, not because it pays. We give cheerfully because *"God is able"* not because of an absolute promise to prosper us. Giving cheerfully is to give for the glory of God and not for our own. The tither should possess the *"but if not"* faith that the three Hebrew children possessed when they were told if they did not bow down before King Nebuchadnezzar's golden image they would be thrown into the firery furnace. They said: *"Our God whom we serve is able to deliver us from the firery furnace, and He will deliver us out of thine hand, O king. But if not, be it known unto thee, O King, that we will not serve thy gods, nor worship the golden image which thou hast set up."* (Daniel 3:16-18) The tither's faith must be exactly like that. Our God is able to bless us, even make us prosper abundantly because we take Him at His word. But if He doesn't, we still know that *"God is able."* In the meantime we will tithe anyway! That is cheerful giving. Does it mean that these promises are absolute guarantees that the cheerful giver will never have a financial reverse? No. Because there are times when God tries us to test our motives. It was said of Hezekiah, *"God left him to test him and to know everything that was in his heart."* (II Chronicles 32:3 NIV). If God seems to hide his face from us for only a season by putting us through economic difficulty — even though we have been tithing — it is to test us to see whether or not we will continue to do exactly as His word tells us to give what is His. . . . *"For God loves (that is, He takes pleasure in, prizes above other things, and is unwilling to abandon or to do without) a cheerful (joyous prompt-to-do-it) giver — whose heart is in his giving."* (Proverbs 9:7 — Amplified Translation)

29. WHY IS SATAN CALLED THE DEVOURER?

Because the Bible says, *"The thief cometh not, but to steal and to kill, and to destroy: I am come that they might have life, and that they might have it more abundantly."* (John 10:10) The function of Satan is to devour. Peter confirms this when he says, *"Be sober be vigilant; because your adversary the devil, as a roaring lion, walketh about, seeking whom he may devour;"* (I Peter 5:8) He is attempting to consume, to eat away at our spiritual vitals and to erode the foundation of our faith. He is not out just to play games, but he is out to kill and to destroy us.

One of the great necessities in any warfare is to know who your real adversary is, and then to know his methods of attack. The scripture tells us that our adversary is the Devil and his method is to attack and devour us.

In the garden when Satan came in he deceived Eve, but Adam wasn't deceived, he went into it with his eyes wide open, that is why the fall came through Adam. So whether we do not tithe because Satan has blinded us or by our own stubborn will or choice, it is still sin, and we will pay the penalty. Man lost all of his rights to God's blessing and recourses in the garden. But through the tithes and offerings He wants to restore His blessings and resources upon His people.

The first statement we read about concerning the rebuking of the devourer, *"Bring all the tithes — the whole tenth of your income — into the storehouse, and prove Me now by it, says the Lord of hosts, if I will not open the windows of Heaven for you and pour you out a blessing, that there shall not be room enough to receive it. And I will rebuke the devourer for your sakes and he shall not destroy the fruits of your ground, neither shall your vine drop its fruit before the time in the field, says the Lord of Hosts. (Malachi 3:10 & 11 — Amplified Translation).*

We will rejoice when we realize that Jesus came not only as our redeemer to redeem our souls, but He also came as our restorer. He came to restore all those things that Satan came to devour and to take away from us. When we realize this, we can also realize that all financial fear and intimidation can be healed through obedient stewardship.

Our giving doesn't depend on our ability
to give, but on His ability to supply.

30. WHAT IS THE DIFFERENCE BETWEEN THE BENEFITS OF SATAN AND OF GOD?

The devil decreases, God increases. The devil steals, God adds. The devil gives evil while God gives righteousness. Satan kills and destroys, but God gives life and life more abundantly.

31. WHY DOES GOD WANT HIS CHILDREN TO HAVE MONEY?

If all the Christians were poor, where would the money come from to propagate the gospel. Money doesn't just drop out of the sky, but rather God uses man to be a channel to give, that the gospel might reach out to the world. We must remember that not only the world belongs to God but all that is in it, therefore as His children it is rightly ours by inheritance.   Proverbs 13:22 *". . . And the wealth of the sinner is laid up for the just."*

32. PROSPERITY SCRIPTURES

Genesis 39:2, 22 & 23
Deuteronomy 28:8-12
Deuteronomy 29:9
Joshua 1:8
I Chronicles 16:29
I Chronicles 29:9
I Chronicles 29:12
I Chronicles 29:14
I Chronicles 29:16 & 17
II Chronicles 1:11 & 12
II Chronicles 26:5
II Chronicles 31:10 & 21
Job 36:9-11
Psalms 1:1-3
Psalms 35:27
Psalms 50:10-15
Psalms 84:11
Psalms 118:25
Proverbs 3:5-10
Proverbs 8:17-21

Proverbs 10:22
Proverbs 11:24 & 25
Proverbs 19:17
Ecclesiastes 5:19
Malachi 3:11 & 12
Matthew 6:33
Mark 4:24
Luke 6:38
Luke 12:31 & 32
John 10:10
John 16:24
Romans 8:32
I Corinthians 16:2
II Corinthians 8:9
II Corinthians 8:12 & 15
II Corinthians 9:6-8
Philippians 4:19
I Timothy 6:17
III John 2

God can do anything — but fail!

33. SOME NOTED TITHERS

Mr. J. C. Penney, owner of the J. C. Penney stores. **Mr. Kraft** of the Kraft Cheese Company started tithing when he was pushing a milk and cheese cart on the streets of New York. **Mr. A. A. Hyde,** owner of Mentholatum. **Mr. Heinz** of the 57 varieties. **Mr. Kerr** of the Kerr Jar Company. **Mr. Proctor** of Ivory Soap. **Mr. Hershey,** of Hershey Chocolate. **Mr. Jarman,** shoe manufacturer. **Mr. Kellogg,** Corn Flakes; and **Mr. Crowell,** of Quaker Oats.

William Colgate of the Colgate shaving cream, toothpaste, etc. started tithing in his youth. One-tenth, two-tenths, three-tenths, four-tenths, five-tenths, and then he saved enough to live on and gave God all of his income. **Maurice K. Jessup, W. M. Baldwin, John H. Converse, Mrs. Russell Sage, Samuel Inslee, William E. Dodge, John Steward Kennedy. Mr. Matthias Baldwin,** founder of the Baldwin Locomotive Industry.

John D. Rockefeller, the financial wizard of the world, began tithing at the age of eight years. He said, "I have tithed on every dollar that God has entrusted to me, and I want to say to you that I could have never tithed on my first million if I had not tithed on my first salary which was $1.50 a week." He became one of the richest men in the world.

When the late **R. G. LeTourneau,** manufacturer of earth-movers and all kinds of heavy equipment accepted Christ, he decided to go into business with God, and everything went fine for several years, but then he got off on the wrong track. He said to himself, "I will take all my finances to handle the program I have set this year, and next year I'll have lots of money for the Lord." He realized later he had been wrong, as he stated in his testimony. It doesn't take much faith to count up what's left and give God a portion of it. God expects us to let Him have the first fruits and trust Him that the harvest will be sufficient to meet the needs, for without faith we are told it is impossible to please Him. You can guess the results. His business went on the verge of financial bankruptcy. He met God again and told God he couldn't give because he didn't have any money, but God encouraged him to renew his covenant and trust Him. Within a few weeks the payroll that had been five weeks behind, was coming through on time. R. G. LeTourneau was a very wealthy man, in heaven as well as on earth. He gave God ninety percent of his income and lived on ten percent. He found God's word, as you will if you try Him, to be true.

34. WHEN THE HEART IS RIGHT, WHAT WILL BE OUR RESPONSE TO TITHING?

1. Tithing is a joy, not a burden.
2. Tithing brings the satisfaction of living for Him and others.
3. Tithing expresses love for God, moves us to praise Him for life.
4. Tithing opens the way to spiritual blessings.
5. Tithing places God in His rightful position — first in mind and life.
6. Tithing puts you in a position where God can truly bless you.
7. Tithing solves money problems, by turning them over to God.
8. Tithing is an act of faith. You may not be able to see how you can afford to tithe, but God has promised to "pour out blessings" upon you if you do. He keeps His promises.
9. Tithing is a test of faith. It proves you are wholly depending upon God, believing in Him, trusting Him with all He has entrusted to you.

You Can't Afford Not to Tithe!

35. COVENANT OF FULFILLMENT.

If you are not a tither, if you will make the same covenant that Jacob did, it will change your life as it did his. Genesis 28:22 "And of all that thou shalt give me I will surely give the tenth unto thee."

The vital step we must take to fulfill the great commandment is "To love the Lord our God with all our heart, with all our soul and with all our mind."

When we submit to His Lordship in every area of our lives, it is then and only then that the complete joy of our Christian life can come into complete fulfillment. It can all be summed up in these words, "Give all to God you would keep for eternity".

Tithing unlocks the door
to God's promises.

Tithing is a golden thread that runs through every book of the Bible, but nowhere is there an indication that the tithe is all a man owes God. It is the minimum, not the maximum . . .

GIVING FROM THE HEART
II Corinthians 9:6-8

K.J.V. But this I say, He which soweth sparingly shall reap also sparingly; and he which sowe bountifully shall reap also bountifully. Every man according as he purposeth in his heart, so him give; not grudgingly, or of necessity: for God loveth a cheerful giver. And God is able make all grace abound toward you; that ye, always having all sufficiency in all things, may abou to every good work:

R.S.V. The point is this: he who sows sparingly will also reap sparingly, and he who sows bou tifully will also reap bountifully. Each one must do as he has made up his mind, not reluctantly under compulsion, for God loves a cheerful giver. And God is able to provide you with ev blessing in abundance, so that you may always have enough of everything and may provide abundance for every good work.

PHILLIPS All I shall say is that poor sowing means a poor harvest, and generous sowing me a generous harvest. Let everyone give as his heart tells him, neither grudgingly nor under co pulsion, for God loves the man who gives cheerfully. After all, God can give you everyth that you need, so that you may always have sufficient both for yourselves and for giving away other people.

N.E.B. Remember: sparse sowing, sparse reaping; sow bountifully, and you will reap bountifu Each person should give as he has decided for himself; there should be no reluctance, no ser of compulsion; God loves a cheerful giver. And it is in God's power to provide you richly w every good gift; thus you will have ample means in yourselves to meet each and every situati with enough and to spare for every good cause.

LIVING BIBLE But remember this, that if you give little you will get little. A farmer who pla just a few seeds will get only a small crop, but if he plants much, he will reap much. Every c must make up his own mind as to how much he should give. Don't force anyone to give m than he really wants to, for cheerful givers are the ones God prizes. God is able to make it to you by giving you everything you need and more, so that there will not only be enough your own needs, but plenty left over to give joyfully to others.

AMPLIFIED Remember this: he who sows sparingly and grudgingly will also reap sparingly a grudgingly, and he who sows generously and that blessings may come to someone, will a reap generously and with blessings. Let each one give as he has made up his own mind a purposed in his heart, not reluctantly or sorrowfully or under compulsion, for God loves (tha He takes pleasure in, prizes above above other things, and is unwilling to abandon or to without) a cheerful (joyous, prompt-to-do-it) giver — whose heart is in his giving. And Go able to make all grace (every favor and earthly blessing) come to you in abundance, so t you may always and under all circumstances and whatever the need, be self-sufficient — possess enough to require no aid or support and furnished in abundance for every good work and ch table donation.

If you do not like to give,
THEN INVEST!
It will reap benefits